# Worth-Focused Design, Book 1

*Balance, Integration, and Generosity*

# Synthesis Lectures on Human-Centered Informatics

Editor
**John M. Carroll**, *Penn State University*

Human-Centered Informatics (HCI) is the intersection of the cultural, the social, the cognitive, and the aesthetic with computing and information technology. It encompasses a huge range of issues, theories, technologies, designs, tools, environments, and human experiences in knowledge work, recreation and leisure activity, teaching and learning, and the potpourri of everyday life. The series publishes state-of-the-art syntheses, case studies, and tutorials in key areas. It shares the focus of leading international conferences in HCI.

Worth-Focused Design, Book 1: Balance, Integration, and Generosity
Gilbert Cockton

Usabiity Testing: A Practitioner's Guide to Evaluating the User Experience
Morten Hertzum

Geographical Design: Spatial Cognition and Geographical Information Science, Second Edition
Stephen C. Hirtle

Human-Computer Interactions in Museums
Eva Hornecker and Luigina Ciolfi

Encounters with HCI Pioneers: A Personal History and Photo Journal
Ben Shneiderman

Social Media and Civic Engagement: History, Theory, and Practice
Scott P. Robertson

The Art of Interaction: What HCI Can Learn from Interactive Art
Ernest Edmonds

Representation, Inclusion, and Innovation: Multidisciplinary Explorations
Clayton Lewis

Research in the Wild
Yvonne Rogers and Paul Marshall

Worth-Focused Design, Book 1: Balance, Integration, and Generosity
Gilbert Cockton

ISBN: 978-3-031-01101-6     print
ISBN: 978-3-031-02229-6     ebook
ISBN: 978-3-031-00209-0     hardcover

DOI 10.1007/978-3-031-02229-6

A Publication in the Springer series
*SYNTHESIS LECTURES ON HUMAN-CENTERED INFORMATICS*
Lecture #46
Series Editor: John M. Carroll, Penn State University

Series ISSN   1946-7680  Print    1946-7699  Electronic

# Worth-Focused Design, Book 1

*Balance, Integration, and Generosity*

Gilbert Cockton
University of Sunderland

*SYNTHESIS LECTURES ON HUMAN-CENTERED INFORMATICS #46*

## ABSTRACT

This book will develop an appropriate common language for truly interdisciplinary teams involved in design. Design now has many meanings. For some, it is the creation of value. For others, it is the conception and creation of artefacts. For still others, it is fitting things to people. These differences reflect disciplinary values that both overlap and diverge. All involve artefacts: we always design things. Each definition considers people and purpose in some way. Each handles evaluation differently, measuring against aesthetics, craft standards, specifications, sales, usage experiences, or usage outcomes. There are both merits and risks in these differences, without an appropriate balance. Poor balance can result from professions claiming the centre of design for their discipline, marginalising others. Process can also cause imbalance when allocating resources to scheduled stages. Balance is promoted by replacing power centres with power sharing, and divisive processes with integrative progressions. A focus on worth guides design towards worthwhile experiences and outcomes that generously exceed expectations.

This book places worth focus (Wo-Fo) into the context of design progressions that are balanced, integrated, and generous (BIG). BIG and Wo-Fo are symbiotic. Worth provides a focus for generosity. Effective worth-focused design requires BIG practices. The companion book *Worth-Focused Design, Book 2: Approaches, Contexts, and Case Studies* (Cockton, 2020b) relates the concept of worth to experiences and outcomes based on a number of practical case studies.

## KEYWORDS

design theory, design research, creative practice, design process, design management, critical creative design, design reflection, design planning

# Contents

# Preface

Computers are now everywhere, supporting websites, in mobile devices, on desktops, and in public information systems, ticket sales kiosks, home appliances, in car-systems, and much more. Our digital age can feel radically different to previous ones, but continuities reach back decades, centuries, and even millenia. For example, the many professions involved in design and development of digital artefacts all predate computers in some way. Visual designers have been with us for millenia, engineers for several centuries, and modern professional (business) managers for around one century. Human factors (ergonomics) barely predate the invention of the stored program computer approximately seven decades ago. Professions bring value systems that shape both their attitudes towards design and also their expectations for design practice. These value-driven expectations begin with education and are refined and reinforced by the professional bodies that steadily superseded craft organisations during the Industrial Revolution.

Design is inherently *axiological* (Biedenbach and Jacobsson, 2016): value trumps fact. Disciplines that construct themselves as objectively value-neutral cause friction in multi-disciplinary settings, as they lack the critical reflective practices that expose and acknowledge unavoidable value orientations.

Broadly speaking, three major value systems mould software design, respectively prioritising desirability, capability, and rationality. The first had its roots in pre-industrial craft traditions, but broadened in modern Schools of Art and Design to consider aesthetics in the context of manufacturing for mass markets. The second had its roots in the Scientific Revolution, and focused on technical considerations, for example in British Mechanics Institutes, which evolved into university Engineering departments. The third major value system has its roots in Scientific Management, as initially taught in Colleges of Commerce (UK) and similar educational institutions worldwide. Each value system spans distinct educational and professional practices.

Initially, computers were the domain of engineers, focused mostly on hardware at first, and then increasingly on software. Once computers became important commercial and administrative tools, business schools developed Management Information Systems as a subdiscipline. Once consumer markets developed for hardware, software, and computer services, established management disciplines such as marketing and innovation extended their interest to digital products and services. With digital convergence for all existing audio-visual media, design and media educators and professionals extended their interests and expertise into multimedia and interaction design (IxD).

Professionals and educators in engineering, management, and design have distinct value systems. There are overlaps between, and differences within, each group of professional values.

However, their different respective core values of capability, rationality, and desirability shape how design work is understood and practiced. At the risk of oversimplification:

- engineering seeks demonstrable solutions (preferably optimal) to clearly specified problems;

- management stresses outcomes, with digital artefacts judged by their value achieved through ownership and use by organisations and individuals; and

- creative design stresses delight and appreciation, with consumers being surprised by, admiring, and enjoying outstanding imagination and realisation.

While optimal solutions, achieved value, and audience delight can and do overlap, it is possible (and very common) for one or two to be achieved without the other. Engineers can thus solve a challenging technical problem in ways that have no obvious value for any human activity, and do not excite possible consumers. Similarly, designers can be outstandingly original and creative but fail to properly consider user needs or technical realities. Also, management strategists can become fixated on new product or service propositions for which there can be no viable technical and/or creative realisation in any foreseeable future.

Brown (2009) has framed design thinking as something that "brings together what is desirable from a human point of view with what is technologically feasible and economically viable," but this aspiration is not systematically met in practice. Unfortunately, current approaches to developing digital products and services tend to be firmly rooted in one value system. Engineering design approaches focus on systematic approaches to problem analysis, requirements specification, and design and analysis of solutions. Management approaches focus on business cases and value propositions. Creative design can develop radically novel artefacts that previously had not been envisaged. However, any single "centre" for design makes it hard to balance capability, rationality, and desirability. However, a hybrid methodology that aims to blend the best of disjoint value systems will introduce new problems of integration across different professional work streams.

## TAKING LEAVE OF OUR CENTRES

My career has repeatedly cycled me through three disciplinary value systems. As a high school teacher, I designed and implemented e-learning systems to achieve educational outcomes. As a freelance programmer, I wrote computer games to delight. As a computer science researcher, I sought systematic approaches to the design and specification of interactive systems, which became the basis for my teaching on undergraduate computing degrees. As a user-centred design researcher, I worked with research groups to develop novel approaches to designing for contexts of use (Cockton and Clarke, 1999) and evaluating quality in use (Cockton et al., 2003; McDonald et al., 2006). As the director of support projects for a region's digital sector, I worked with business owners and senior managers to deliver value to a rapidly growing cluster of digital service providers and their value chains. As I followed their lead to think in terms of value propositions, I became critical of user-centred design (UCD) and its foci on quality in use and fit to context. While both of these could be engineered, assisted by creative flair, the choice of evaluation targets felt arbitrary without understanding the rationale for a digital product or service in terms of the value that it should deliver (Cockton, 2004a, 2004b).

A solution was obvious: stop centring on users and usage and, instead, centre on value. This radically new value-centred design (VCD) would focus on the value achieved during and after use of a digital product or service. This was later extended to worth-centred design (WCD). The broader concept of *worth* better captures the balance between positive and negative values (Cockton, 2006). As I was moving from users and usage to value and worth, John Heskett was moving his graduate seminar on Design and the Creation of Value with him from Chicago to Hong Kong (Dilnot, 2017). However, Heskett and I had different aims.

Heskett sought to improve design's ability to demonstrate how it creates and adds value by drawing on economic theory, although for Dilnot (2017, p.11), Heskett "never conflates 'economic value' with value or values per se." Interestingly, his focus on economic value was often turned to other perspectives on value and values (Heskett, 2017, Appendix B).

My aim was practice-based. I sought to improve design teams' understanding of value (or better still, worth) and their ability to make explicit use of their understanding when designing interactive systems. I was able to build on my undergraduate and postgraduate studies in history, philosophy, psychology, and sociology. Heskett and I ended up with similar positions but with very different disciplinary balances. However, we were focused on different audiences and purposes: demonstrating design's overall value as a professional practice in economic terms (Heskett); designing for specific worth for specific digital products or services. In Frayling's (1993) terms, Heskett was carrying out research *into* design, and I was carrying out research *for* design.

Over the previous decade, I had become intermittently aware of the nature of creative design practices, with their roots in the new Art and Design Schools of the Industrial Revolution. I had based much of a Master's design course that I taught in 1996 on Lawson's (1980) research into creative design practices, with a clear focus on the concurrent nature of creative design activities, in contrast to the sequential stages of idealised engineering design (iteration preserves sequence). As a UK NESTA fellow from 2005–2008, I was mentored by two distinguished design researchers and educators, reawakening my interest in creative design practice. However, even towards the end of this fellowship, when I spent three months at Microsoft Research Cambridge, I failed to support concurrent creative practices (Cockton et al., 2009a). Centring on worth was effective for integrating across completed design work on a digital Family Archive, but not for directing, balancing, and scheduling additional work.

Unsurprisingly, any design methodology with a single centre is biased in ways that obstruct the balance of activities that best suits a specific project. I began to explore balance through the concepts of design choices within Abstract Design Situations (Cockton, 2009a, 2010b), which involved four different *design arenas* (Cockton, 2013a, 2013b). Arenas are worked on concurrently in different episodes of design work, with shifting foci instead of a single "centre" for design. Worth is only a focus within the *design purpose* arena. This evolved worth-centred design into a balanced *worth-focused* (Wo-Fo) approach with integration across four design arenas. My Ph.D. student Jenni George developed a family of representations for Abstract Design Situations that are used to track, reflect, and plan during design work (George, 2016).

Concurrent work on design arenas lets creative design-led activities go beyond known needs, wants, desires, and dreams of identified beneficiaries to more *generous* approaches to design purpose. Design could thus be BIG—Balanced, Integrated, and Generous—by balancing design activities across a project and also integrating these activities in ways that left room for creative opportunities alongside well-grounded insights about beneficiaries.

Changing design's centre from users via value to worth was less effective than supporting multiple foci, being Wo-Fo some but not all of the time (and actually, not much of the time relatively). Multiple changing integrated foci increase the manageable complexity of factors under consideration during design. Rather than:

- placing all our trust in a single centre (such as users, usage, value, values or worth), BIG expects and supports multiple dynamic foci; and

- focusing predominantly on positive or negative outcomes, a Wo-Fo considers the balance of both, based on the understanding that positives can outweigh, or compensate for, negatives.

Such complexity may feel very challenging, with so many factors under consideration. A key aim of this book is to communicate how such complexity can be managed and, thus, avoid the (often unacceptable) compromises that methodologies with centres and fixed processes (such as UCD) impose on design teams. BIG design combines existing perspectives from UCD, VCD, and WCD. The last two are variants of UCD, but BIG design subsumes them all. User-focused UCD and user experience (UX) practices co-exist alongside (or either side of) Wo-Fo and design-led practices.

## WHO SHOULD READ THIS BOOK?

This book is for everyone who is aware in any way of limitations of current approaches to IxD at their current career stage. Students or professionals working within constraining engineering or innovation ("design thinking") methodologies can learn how to open up their work to more creative practices while maintaining a focus on worthwhile experiences and outcomes. Similarly, designers working in loosely structured practices such as Agile development or unconstrained exploratory design can learn how to add useful and productive structure to their work, especially a clear sense of design purpose coupled with the ability to ground this in understandings of beneficiaries and evaluations of usage. Managers and directors can learn practices and perspectives that take them beyond the limitations of current design thinking, design led, agile, and lean practices and improve their tracking, scheduling, and subtle direction of concurrent design work.

I see reading as an active process and writing as a resource to prompt reflection, criticism, questions, and deliberation. I thus use a mix of writing styles in this book, building on experimental writing for the ACM CHI conference alt.chi track that has used drama form (Cockton, 2008d), parody (Cockton, 2012a, 2012b), and humanities-influenced critique (Cockton, 2008b, 2013c, 2017). While styles of technical writing have much to commend them, they are inherently conservative and too often write to avoid active reading (e.g., reflection, deliberation, questions, critical responses). The situated nature of design means that design teams must be able to relate what they have read to their projects. The cookbook extreme of technical writing is thus unsuitable for this book's content. Even its more technical parts of this book are written to prompt reflection, criticism, questions, and deliberation. Where easing up a technical writing style is not enough to expose the limitations of current orthodoxies for software design, I have used fiction, extending current design fiction work from envisioning future artefacts to fictions on design practice and research. I have done this to put creative values on an equal footing with technical ones through the creative use of language. Being open to creative practice is helped by being open to creative writing.

I also see both reading and writing as a critical process, where close attention to language is needed to expose hidden assumptions and masked *lacunae* (gaps). Inadequate conservative approaches to design from engineering and human-centred practices are often spared critical examination through the use of language that appeals to rational value systems such as Scientism and Bureaucratism.

## LETTING GO WITHOUT LOSING YOUR GRIP

Our education socialises us into disciplinary value systems that are reproduced through professional practices. Employers and customers also bring their own value systems. Successful design depends on being able to let go of strong socialised value orientations to thoroughly explore new perspectives. It also depends on being able to persuade employers and customers, too, that they will benefit from being more open to innovative design practices beyond the commoditised packaging of Design Thinking, UCD, Engineering Design Management, and similar "answer-to-everything" approaches. Instead, we need to develop competences, expertise, and principles that maintain and develop a "palette" (Friedland, 2019) that supports a wide range of demanding projects and stakeholders, given structure for specific contexts as possible within a "playbook" (Gajander, 2019).

One advantage of focusing on worth in design is that it applies to the process as much as the outcomes of design. If we are generous with our beneficiaries as designers, then we must also be generous with our own design processes. We need to understand what is worthwhile about a range of disciplinary and professional practices. We then need to take the best of each and reduce their drawbacks. Benefits can make drawbacks worthwhile, but when drawbacks are reduced or even removed, design practices become even more worthwhile.

Thinking in terms of worth means that we must assess both the positives and negatives of specific disciplinary and professional practices and respond appropriately. As designers, we primarily serve others and not our disciplines or professions. We need to be able to critically reflect on the values into which we have been socialised by education or professional practice. We should be comfortable with having our values challenged and be able to assess their impact on our design practices. We need a strong grip on how we get design work to work, and that means letting go of values when they do not demonstrably translate into effective actions.

With an undergraduate degree in Humanities, a post-graduate certificate in Education, a Ph.D. in Computing Science, and a UK NESTA fellowship for design research, I have no one disciplinary loyalty, which makes me stand back from my writing as it develops. Most of this book draws on Software Engineering and Interaction Design, but my Humanities and Applied Human Science backgrounds spawn critical responses. I thus found myself looking for a deeper underpinning of the practice-based work in this book. This search has been as creative as the practice-based work that it sought to critique, so unsurprisingly my position on the unavoidable risks of creative work eventually had me rendezvous with theories and frameworks from social approaches to risk (Beck, 1992; Renn, 2008). Surprisingly, though, some key positions there turned out to resonate strongly with the tensions between creative and rational design that this book seeks to tame. Ultimately, an effective rendezvous between the creative and the rational is about understanding and managing risk. Both "camps" in design have strengths and weaknesses that must be recognised and responded to.

Gilbert Cockton
April 2020

# Acknowledgements

This book has its roots over 25 years ago in the work of my first two Computing Ph.D. students at Glasgow University. Steven Clarke responded to second wave HCI (Rogers et al., 1993) by exploring the nature of links (connections, in this book) between contextual research into beneficiaries and the design of software artefacts. He moved away from assumptions of synchronised clean interfaces between phases of software development cycles to incremental asynchronous connections. Darryn Lavery developed methodological resources for the systematic study of evaluation work that was to develop into a resource-based approach to design work.

Ph.D. students and colleagues in computing at Sunderland University built on this research from 1997–2009. Alan Woolrych and Mark Hindmarch developed an understanding of informative and expressive resources in evaluation work. Sharon McDonald and Kelly Monahan demonstrated the flexibility of UCD methods by repurposing contextual research approaches for evaluation. Alongside this continuing work on evaluation, specialised approaches and resources for contextual research were developed for accessibility (Eamon Doherty, Paul Gnanayutham, Brendan Cassidy), culture (Fuad AL Qirem), and e-learning (Susan Jones).

From 1999–2005, I directed regional support projects for the digital sector in the northeast of England. Industrial board members on three projects improved my understanding of business strategy and made me more aware of the limitations of UCD approaches to contextual research and usability evaluation in the broader context of developing and marketing digital products and services. I thus chose to focus VCD for the UK NESTA fellowship that I was awarded from 2005–2008. I had the very good fortune to be mentored by Gillian Crampton-Smith. Gillian and her husband, Phil Tabor, developed my understanding of perspectives from creative design education and research. During this fellowship, I was seconded to Microsoft Research Cambridge and was an international advisor to the Finnish TEKES VALU project. At Microsoft, Abigail Sellen, David Kirk, and Richard Banks were particularly helpful with the development of worth sketching and mapping, which Sari Kujala, and Piia Nurkka developed further on the VALU project. I developed a range of Wo-Fo resources during my NESTA fellowship.

The rejection of fixed design and evaluation methods, and their reconceptualization as approaches and resources, developed during two European COST networks, MAUSE and TwinTide, with applications in consultancy as part of the regional CODEWORKS digital support project. Resource functions underpinned work by my Ph.D. students in Northumbria University's School of Design from 2010 onwards. Malcolm Jones discovered multiple resource functions (rather than types) in his Ph.D. on storytelling resources (Jones, 2020). Jenni George's Ph.D. applied a wide range of new design theory to a Wo-Fo case study (George, 2016).

Stuart English, Bob Young, and Matt Lievesley introduced me to some of the key references on creative design work in Northumbria's former Centre for Design Research, where Louise Taylor and Joyce Yee invented what I call Why-Frames in Cockton (2020b, Chapter 4).

The research framework that was refined within the TwinTide project and by Ph.D. students has been the basis for teaching undergraduate and postgraduate students in Italy, Slovenia, Iceland, and the Netherlands. It has also been the basis for workshops and courses at conferences in Finland, Germany, Estonia, U.S., Sweden, Canada, and the UK. I have gained much from the hundreds of participants on these courses. My framework has also been extended in response to several Ph.D.s that I have examined, and collaborations arising within the TwinTide COST network, in particular with Kasper Hornbæk, Erik Frøkjær, Marcin Sikorski, Igor Garnik, Marta Lárusdóttir, and Åsa Cajander.

This book is thus the result of dozens of collaborations and several funded projects. I have also benefitted from independent use of the approaches that I have developed, as covered in Cockton (2020b, Chapter 6). I have been very fortunate to have received advice, ideas, knowledge, and guidance from a wide range of colleagues in academia and business, as well as the trust and enthusiasm of colleagues who have independently applied my approaches. Most recently as Co-Editor-in-Chief of ACM *Interactions* magazine, I have had the opportunity to interact with colleagues at all stages of their careers, which has refreshed and extended the framework presented here.

Gilbert Cockton
April 2020

CHAPTER 1

# Three Years In: A Design Practice Fiction

It's been three years since CloudBooks was launched. It's a Software as a Service product for managing a small company's accounts, with additional support for setting up, running, and growing a businesses. Customers access it through a web interface in return for an annual subscription. CloudBooks is developed using an Agile development process, with bi-weekly updates to the live system. There are a few dozen professionals working on CloudBooks, spanning marketing, product management, software development, product support, and user experience. Product management are focused on future strategy, but will answer questions and give feedback on current work items. The team has planned activities for the next months at different levels of detail. For the next two weeks, the developers and their interaction design (IxD) team know the detailed design and implementation tasks for the current sprint and the user experience (UX) team is working on a range of multidisciplinary activities.

The UX team lead has some customer visits planned, where she will find out about how CloudBooks is being used, what is found most valuable, what difficulties customers experience, and what revisions and extensions would be attractive. The usability evaluation lead has some test sessions arranged with members of their user panel. He will be gathering evidence in relation to user feedback from different support channels, after which he will inspect the user interface designs for the next sprint. The three Interaction Designers are working on two tasks: pixel perfect user interface design for the next sprint, and prototyping some new capabilities in support of the product road map, which will be demonstrated to visitors to the company's stand at an upcoming trade show.

CloudBooks is not a real product, but there are ones like it. The imaginary example above exposes the realities of work on versions of software after its first release. The CloudBooks team are working across four distinct areas of design, which each bring their own development activities and require specific professional expertise in creative design, software design and engineering, product strategy, user research, or usability evaluation (Table 1.1). The first design area focuses on *development* of a complex software artefact, CloudBooks. The second concerns current and future product *strategy*. The third carries out *evaluations* of CloudBooks at various stages of development. The fourth develops understandings of CloudBook's *users*. There's nothing radical in these work patterns. The interleaving of design, coding, planning, hypothesis testing, information gathering, strategic goal setting, and other activities is what we would expect for a mature product. It would be highly inefficient to queue work for each design area, e.g., making development work wait for evaluation results, having strategic reviews wait for completion of a prototype, and delaying customer visits, prototype planning and demonstrations, and evaluation until a current sprint ends.

| Table 1.1: Two weeks of work in four design areas by the CloudBooks team | | |
|---|---|---|
| **Design Area** | **Week 1 Activities** | **Week 2 Activities** |
| Development | Implement user stories for next sprint Prototype new capabilities from CloudBooks road map | |
| Strategy | Answer queries from Interaction Designers about current CloudBooks road map while framing future product strategy | |
| Evaluation | Usability work in response to customer feedback | Usability and wider UX inspection of user interface design for next sprint |
| User Research | Planned customer visits | Plan demonstrations and insight gathering procedures for upcoming trade show |

At the same time, there is no clear co-ordination across design areas here. The team are working on the current, next, and as yet unscheduled versions of CloudBooks simultaneously. It is not clear how evaluation work feeds into other design areas. It is less clear whether questions to Product Management from the Interaction Designers will lead to tweaks, or perhaps more, to the CloudBooks road map. It is even less clear whether findings from the customer visits will have any impact on the other three design areas. Least clear of all (understandably) is the eventual impact of the demonstrations at the upcoming trade show.

These difficulties of co-ordination can be expressed diagrammatically, as in Figure 1.1. The top-left diagram illustrates lack of clear co-ordination from evaluation work to the other areas of design work. The top-right shows a lack of clarity on the impact on product strategy of questions from development about it. The bottom-left shows lack of co-ordination from user research to other design areas. The bottom-right shows a more complex lack of co-ordination from a demonstration via its evaluation to the other design areas.

The work patterns here are thus understandable, but perhaps not ideal. If so, this raises the question as to what would be ideal. It also raises questions about whether these work patterns should ever be different, even when developing the first release of a software product or service. This book addresses these and other questions in depth. It seeks to continue the agile shift from formal engineering design and development sequences to more open and creative practices.

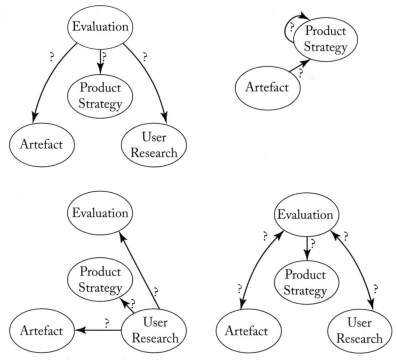

Figure 1.1: Lack of explicit co-ordination in CloudBooks design work.

## 1.1   HOW THIS BOOK CHALLENGES STRONGLY ESTABLISHED POSITIONS

This is the first book of two on having a worth focus (Wo-Fo) in IxD. The second book addresses this Wo-Fo in detail. This first book develops a context that enables a Wo-Fo in design by developing a framework for critical creative design practices. The second book builds on this by covering design approaches and resources that focus on *worthwhile* usage. These are addressed in Book 2, along with approaches and resources for other foci in IxD and approaches to integration across all foci. Book 2 has two chapters on case studies of these approaches in use in a broad framework for critical creative design and evaluation practices

This first book challenges some strongly established disciplinary and professional ideals. This introduction, with the Preface, provides an overview and motivation for this book. The Preface describes the origins and development of the research covered in this book, which draws on three decades of human-centred practices in conjunction with creative, business, and engineering approaches. This chapter began with a *design practice fiction* to which some later chapters will refer. It relates how software design teams do not follow textbook development processes from software engineering and human-centred design, as well as augmenting creative studio practices.

Both books are focused on IxD, but the first is mostly general, and develops theory that applies to other design practices. The foundations for better integration of existing design paradigms lie in understanding and accepting:

- the key realities of creative design work and

- the insurmountable limitations of engineering project management approaches, even in their agile and "Design Thinking" manifestations.

Better integration than that found in current practices can be achieved via comprehensive design situations that can be modelled at varying levels of abstraction in ways that support the effective integration of currently separate design practices. Such modelling can be both theoretically informed and practically applicable

This book extends design fictions to design practice and design research. Fictitious examples are used to let a range of values and paradigms be introduced in ways that prompt readers to reflect on how different disciplinary and professional practices can look from the outside, as well as on what an honest appraisal looks like from the inside. Most of this book takes more well-established approaches to research writing, combining analyses of literature with development of concepts and theories that lend themselves to practical realisations.

This book continues with Chapter 2, which looks at what five decades of research into creative design practice tell us about the structure of design work. After that, Chapter 3 uses a design research fiction to explore how engineering and management values gave rise to normative development processes that have a poor fit to the empirical realities summarised in Chapter 2.

Common ground between ideals, realities, and possibilities that are superficially incompatible is made possible through the concept of *Design Arenas*, a formalisation of Heskett's (2005) position on the origins of design outcomes. Chapter 4 builds on the concepts of design arenas to form a superordinate concept of Abstract Design Situations (ADS) that can be used to scope design work at all levels of abstraction from paradigms, via processes, organisations, projects, phases, and methods down to work resources and even brief design moves. ADS can be used to track and plan design work from inception onwards. Chapter 5 relates Chapter 2's understandings of creative design practices to ADS, by showing how a partially planned development process can be tracked and replanned using design arenas and ADS concepts. These chapters develop a new lexicon for design progressions, replacing the proceses and phases of idealised normative engineering design. A glossary is used in both books to gather this new lexicon in one place.

Chapter 6 concludes this book with a summary of a new approach to design paradigms that values balance, integration, and generosity rather than centres, processes, and delivering to specification. In the second book, the focus shifts to practical IxD. Chapter 5 provides a bridge from this book's theory to the practice of the second book.

## 1.2    WHAT IS IMPORTANT ABOUT HOW THE CLOUDBOOKS TEAM WORKS

The CloudBooks team's story is simple. They work as they do because this is how all creatives work. They did not sleepwalk into the chaos of a parallel process with multiple concurrent design activities, with reflective pauses for integration and forward planning and strategy. Instead, they always work this way from project inception onwards. There is never a "big upfront" analysis and specification at the outset, and no fixed iterative cycle of analysis, synthesis, and evaluation. They are more agile than any published Agile methodology. Although they work creatively, the CloudBooks team are not a loose collection of independent creative prima donnas. Their work is often shaped by user- or market-focused activities, but is primarily driven forward by a strong product strategy, understandings of a broad range of trends (creative, business, and technological) and the creative confidence required to pull all these disparate design inputs together. The team do not follow a single process and methodology. Instead, they leverage a continuously evolving "palette" of design resources and approaches (Friedland, 2019), some of which are combined into a "playbook" of set piece design processes for common project contexts (Gajander, 2019).

The CloudBooks team's work raises some important questions despite its fictitious nature.

1. What are the main areas of design work? Can it reasonably be divided up in some way (as in Table 1.1)? What are the alternatives to the areas in Table 1.1?

2. How do design work areas relate to each other? How are they connected? What sort of transitions are made as areas are connected?

3. Are there standard process structures that can organise design work without regimenting it into a sequence of phases? How much iteration is needed? How much concurrency can be handled simultaneously? Is there a correct structure?

The goal of this book is to answer these questions in ways that move beyond failed dreams of exclusively rational evidence-based design methodologies to ones that are more open, and take realistic approaches to balancing the creative realities of design work, based on palettes that support multiple "play" tactics for rigorously combining and information with creative design work. After reviewing research into creative design in the next chapter and seeing how much of the above can be answered with it, Chapter 3 returns with a design research fiction that will add further questions to those above.

CHAPTER 2

# The Realities of Creative Design Practice

The CloudBooks' story in Chapter 1 is a design practice fiction. Even so, we can ask whether it is typical of software development practice. Alternatively, we could ask if it conforms to relevant standards. The main international standard for Human-Centred Design (HCD) is ISO 9241-210 (ISO, 2019a; Figure 2.1), which began as the earlier ISO13407 standard, with a previous version in 2012. It is the basis for a major ongoing UX certification initiative (uxqb.org).

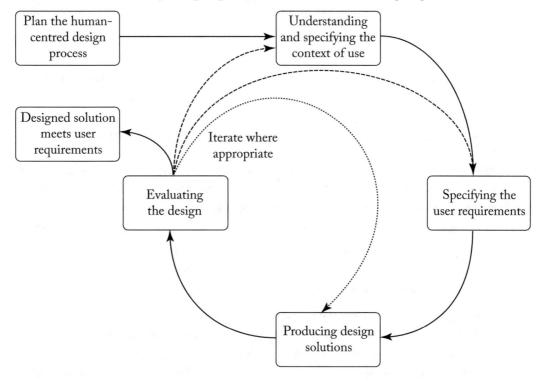

Figure 2.1: HCD process for ISO 9241-210 (example resources on solid arrows omitted).

ISO 9241-210 is a linear process where each phase has a single work focus. A phase's output is input to the next: nothing else is needed. Simple arrows represent routine transitions between phases. Updates since ISO13407 have not changed the linear nature of this process model. In

2012, two extra iteration transitions (dashed) were added post evaluation. There was just the dotted transition in Figure 2.1 in ISO13407. Rather than repeat a full "waterfall" cycle of four main development phases for every iteration, following evaluation development can continue with any other phase. Even so, all iterative processes are sequential in underlying structure, with no concurrent phases (Fallman, 2003). Iteration only makes sense for sequential processes. It is meaningless for concurrent ones. Interestingly, Jones (1970) "designer as computer model" has one feedback link from evaluation to analysis (top "understand" box in Figure 2.1 and possibly its requirements box too), so iteration fashions very over time.

The CloudBooks team's processes are nothing like ISO9241-210, which is unrealistic and riddled with gaps that have remained unacknowledged for the two decades of it and its predecessor. It does not match how creative design work actually happens in practice, as consistently revealed by over 50 years of research into creative design practice. The next section reviews this to show why the CloudBooks process cannot be like ISO9241-210.

After this review, 50 years of research into creative design practice are expressed as three key realities of creative design practice, which call for a new compatible design work vocabulary. The need for this vocabulary is then considered, followed by reviews of the nature of transitions between work areas in creative design and understandings of creative work in HCI research.

## 2.1    A HALF CENTURY OF RESEARCH INTO DESIGN

Early design research was normative, like ISO 9241-210 today. It was *research for design* (Frayling, 1993) that set standards, irrespective of realities. It aimed to improve creative design work by making it better informed, and more systematic and rational. Creative expertise and judgement were seen as impeding more scientific practices, such as human factors and ergonomics. Difficulties in scientifically informing design-led engineers such as Bruce Archer (Royal College of Art, UK) and John Chris Jones (Associated Electrical Industries then UMIST, UK) to propose systematic approaches. In the Preface to the second edition of Jones' *Design Methods*, he was quoted:

> *I didn't want to get involved with design theory or methods … I did this ergonomic study of how the designing was done purely with the view of getting the ergonomic information, which was obviously sound and well tested, into the engineering design process at the point where it wouldn't be rejected, … in doing that I hit on what's now called design methods* (Mitchell, 1992).

Note that Jones began with research *into* design (Frayling, 1993) to establish why his ergonomic information was not used at the right "point" in an engineering design process. He followed through with research for design, proposing a systematic design method as a solution to his problems. Research for design dominated the first decade of design research, but with very limited success (Jones, 1988), resulting in a shift to research *into* design. Even though Jones had studied engineering design practice before proposing his systematic design method, there was clearly some form of disconnect between the actual problem and Jones' solution. The middle decades of design research focused on understanding how designers actually worked, with no preconceived notions that design work was scientifically problematic and had to be fixed.

Today there are many published first- and second-hand accounts of creative design work, e.g., focusing on Software Design (Petre and van der Hoek, 2016), Product Design and related practices (Dorst, 2017), Advertising (Hegarty, 2014), and creative arts in general (Al-Maria et al., 2016). These four publications are well-designed easy reads with simple spreads, short essays, and discussions to quickly communicate the diversity of creative practice. There is much in common across the professional practices covered, and it is this core creative practice that is our first basis for identifying common realities of creative practice. Dorst (2015) proposed five lessons from design:

1. Co-evolution

2. Developing problem situations

3. Handling frames

4. Exploiting themes

5. Fostering a discourse

## 2.1.1   CO-EVOLUTION

In creative design work, problem and solution spaces co-evolve. They are not worked on separately in fixed sequences. An early recognition of this was Rittel and Webber's (1973) account of "wicked problems," which cannot be not finally framed until a solution is accepted. ISO 9241-210, like most rational methodologies, expects a problem to be analysed and requirements specified before design work begins. Rittel and Webber, however, were not the first to note that "a vast variety of design decisions cannot be taken … before the solution in principle is known, conjecture and problem specification thus proceed side-by-side rather than in sequence" (Hillier et al., 1972).

Interestingly, Rittel and Webber presented wicked problems as a policy problem (in particular for urban planning) and not as fundamental to creative practice. It was almost two decades before Dorst and other design researchers located "wickedness" in creative practice rather than in (just) the world. By letting problem and solution spaces continuously co-evolve, creative designers acknowledge the impossibility of completely closing on the exact nature of a problem without giving substantial consideration to possible solutions. Curent leading edge design research practices such as *Annotated Portfolios* (Gaver and Bowers, 2012) make co-evolution explicitly symbiotic, with artefacts illuminated by annotations and annotations illustrated by artefacts: "annotations and the designs they annotate are mutually informative."

## 2.1.2    DEVELOPING PROBLEM SITUATIONS

With co-evolution, both problem situations and potential solutions are developed concurrently. Tame problems aside, design teams do not analyse problems and specify requirements once and for all, or in isolation. Instead, understandings of problem situations co-evolve alongside development of possible solutions. Problem situations are open, complex, dynamic, and networked (Dorst, 2015), unlike closed frozen problem definitions. Consequently, problem situations are being continuously developed by design teams, and for Dorst this has more impact on innovation than a focus on solutions. While problems and solutions co-evolve, the framing of problem situations spawns innovation more than the creation of solutions.

## 2.1.3    HANDLING FRAMES

The role of frames may be Dorst's (2015) most important "lesson from design." A creative design team's approach to "a problem" is expressed by a frame. Solutions are also framed, but for Dorst, radical innovation is more strongly associated with imaginative problem framing. For design, it is an old lesson, but one that may not be readily learned elsewhere. Doblin (1978) included *semantic definitions* as a resource for innovation:

> *Consciously switching the semantic description of a product produces new ideas. The word "chair" can cause a mental block by describing a platform 18 inches off the floor with four legs and a back. Changing the product description to "body support" can cause the designer to envision a column of air, a ball of foam, a stick strapped to the back, etc.*

Innovative or not, frames give coherence to problem and solution spaces. They summarise the current understanding of a problem or a preferred solution. For Dorst (2015), a frame can be an organising principle, a coherent set of statements, or a combination of both. Gaver and Bower's (2012) designers' "position statement" can be thought of as a frame, for example "framing older people as curious and engaged" and not "as individuals requiring medical care or assistance."

Co-evolution lets problem frames evolve beyond an initial brief, challenge, or insight to guide development of solutions. For Dorst, frames steer explorations and perceptions, directing intentions and actions. They are original, lively, and draw forth mental imagery across design teams, harmonising the thoughts of stakeholders. Innovation results from realistic frames.

Good frames span and integrate a broad range of issues. They can be hard to communicate, but may trigger "'mini-stories" that open up shared experiences across a team. Frames also must be fresh. If fossilized, they become limiting rationales: when something is a frame is more important than what is in one, i.e., to work as a frame, the timing of its formulation is more important than the content of the formulation. Once a frame is accepted, it can fade as design becomes routine once a problem is tamed.

A problem frame is far more extensive than a problem description or specification. It is not enough to coldly state something. A problem frame must inspire, provoke, captivate, inspire, unite, evoke, elicit, share, and more. Less a *what* than a *when*, a frame is only *when* when its formation leads to emotional, inspirational, and social responses. A problem frame that is *generous* is more likely to trigger the positive responses that elevate a proposal to a frame.

Frames are thus simple concepts with complex consequences in design work, but only when they meet the many challenging demands that Dorst places on them. Coming up with strong frames depend on a design team's ideative repertoire.

A difficulty with Dorst's (2015) position on frames is that he has two. The first is summarised above, and is consistent with a broad literature on research into design. The second is more analytical, and starts with models of reasoning to reach a more constrained position on frames that is not backed up by vast literature. This position comes first in Dorst (2015) and is critiqued in Chapter 4.

### 2.1.4   EXPLOITING THEMES

Co-evolution does not occur in a vacuum. Considerations for frames' scopes are drawn from a pool of possibilities organised around *themes*, which design teams draw on when considering potential frames. Frames bring themes from the background consciousness of a design team to the foreground. They make some themes central to the current framing of a design. Themes span problem and solution, letting considerations of both merge during ideation: "concepts that bridge the human (cultural) domain and the technical or economic realms can be inordinately useful as themes" (Dorst, 2015). Themes are patterns in the world that can aid formation of frames, coming into and out of play as frames co-evolve. However, specific themes are always "there" whether or not they direct frame evolution.

Davies and Talbot's (1987) study of elite UK designers revealed broad ubiquitous themes that were often considered: public/private, individual/collective, past/future, and familiar/unfamiliar. A similar practice was called *placements*, which like categories "have boundaries to shape and constrain meaning, but" unlike categories "are not rigidly fixed and determinate" (Buchanan, 1992). Buchanan uses "intrinsic/extrinsic" as an example placement from the designer Jay Doblin, whose *Innovation, A Cook Book Approach* (1978), discusses other themes such as universalities/peculiarities and good/bad, but does not call any of these placements. Buchanan used this term from rhetoric to contrast flexible design thinking with rigid logical categories.

Themes were used when designers noticed particular coincidences that other people failed to notice, drawing on visual imagery. Thirty-five years later, Gaver and Bowers' (2012) portfolio annotations included themes such as "constraint and openness" and "threshold to the surrounding world." Themes are more abstract than specific designs or the contexts that they are designed for.

Annotations vary in their levels of abstraction and scope. They apply with varying balance to one or more designs, their context of use, or both (Löwgren, 2013).

Themes that dissolve apparent design paradoxes are particularly valuable. Initial paradoxes arising from apparently incompatible stakeholder positions can disappear as more universal human needs and values are considered. Themes capture the underlying phenomena in a situation without prejudgement or oversimplification. Themes hang in the balance, neither positive nor negative, until they come together in new ways. They are not part of a problem or solution space, but are important enigmatic resources in design work.

### 2.1.5    FOSTERING A DISCOURSE

In a ISO 9241-210, each phase follows logically from the next, with a phase's outputs generating, or being translated into, the inputs of the next. There is little need for discourse here, as one phase should set up comprehensively for the next. However, in creative design work, relationships between problems and solutions cannot be like mathematical functions such as generation or translation. Both are too simple. Instead, problems and solutions are in mutual dialogue as part of Schön's (1992) "reflective conversation with the materials of a design situation."

Schön's "conversation with materials" were originally within the context of solo design work such as sketching (where sketches "talk back"). For Dorst (2015), fostering a discourse is primarily social with design teams nudging co evolution forward (sometimes by a considerable distance) through joint reflection on current relationships between problem and solution frames.

Discourses are essential in design work, even when there is a single designer in "reflective conversation with the materials of a design situation." As design teams become more diverse and sometimes conflicted, effective discourses become more challenging. Divided loyalties can result when trying to reconcile the needs of customers with those of a firm (Stevens and Moultrie, 2011).

In this book, design teams are understood broadly to include all involved stakeholders. This is especially important for service and policy design work in the public and third sectors, because providers who implement services must be included in the design team (Junginger, 2017). Also, when using design strategically within an organisation, a "complex interplay of influencers and stakeholders" is involved with design integrating and mediating between professional domains (Stevens and Moultrie, 2011), both inside organizations (e.g., marketing, production) and outside (e.g., suppliers, partners).

### 2.1.6    OTHER SUMMARIES FROM RESEARCH INTO DESIGN

Dorst's (2015) list is one of many from research into design, but it is sufficiently comprehensive to be a good basis for understanding creative design. It foregrounds design practices, i.e., co-evolution, (problem) framing, themes, fostered discourses, which are all at the same level of abstraction. This makes it more useful than other lists.

Items on earlier proposed lists of key design factors are less incisive and focused, e.g., Krippendorf (2005), who lists designers' future orientation, envisaging usage, understanding stakeholders, gathering substantiating evidence, and learning through critical examination to adapt and improve. Similarly, Lawson (1980) presents six generalities that are less action-oriented than Dorst's five. Cross (2011) has a loosely coupled short list at very different levels of abstraction, taking a broad systems view, distinctive problem framing, and designing from first principles. Stevens and Moultrie (2011) offer examples, rather than a comprehensive list, of internal capabilities and resources relevant to design and other sources of competitive advantage that let design practices "safely explore the unknown territory of the future." Their examples are tacit knowledge, corporate culture, and shared vision, a list as heterogeneous as those from Cross and others that is not action oriented.

Nelson and Stolterman (2012) present a more complex four foundations and six fundamentals. While much can be empirically grounded in design practices, this must be unpicked from their normative context. Their foundations and fundamentals provide useful concepts for research *into* design, but must be used selectively and judiciously elsewhere.

Dorst's list thus comes closest to the realities of the *activities* of creative *practice*. It maintains a common level of abstraction, which makes for a coherent model of designer behaviour. It is the most up to date and is aligned with the most recent research. It also emphasizes the tacit nature of design work more than other lists, due to its focus on designers' action rather than their "thinking." Focusing on Dorst takes nothing of importance from the other lists that span 21 years of research into design. However, overlap within his five lessons lets them be reduced to three key realities.

## 2.2    THREE KEY REALITIES OF CREATIVE DESIGN PRACTICES

By reducing overlaps in Dorst's list, we can identify three key realities of creative design practices.

### 2.2.1    CO-EVOLUTION

Dorst's first lesson, co-evolution, corresponds directly to a key reality of creative practice. His next three lessons (developing problem situations, handling frames, exploiting themes) either follow from co-evolution or determine its quality, especially via a problem frame.

Co-evolution underlies "overlapping development phases," one of the six factors in successful Japanese consumer product innovation identified by Takeuchi and Nonaka (1986), which contrasted the *relay* of linear engineering design with the concurrent *scrum* of "overlapping development phases" (thus inspiring Agile's Scrum methodology). A study of elite UK designers (Davies and Talbot 1987) complemented this by noting that creative activities overlap and occur in any order.

Rittel and Webber (1973) contrasted "wicked problems" with "tame" ones, where problems could be confidently framed early in a project, and alternative solutions are well known (one of their ten distinguishing properties of wicked vs. tame problems).

Design work can be routine, even barely creative. Such work is still however design, as solutions must still be drawn and/or specified. However, this is largely design as in the narrow sense of its French root, *dessiner* (to draw). Innovative design, not tame design practices are the focus of this book. Currently, software design work is more innovative than routine.

Rittel and Webber's wicked problems are a key reality of innovative creative practice, unlike the normative models of design work that are barely 75 years old (Eckert and Stacey, 2010), and intended to benefit managers, not designers (e.g., ISO, 2019a). They fit the traditions of scientific management well. However, in addition to what we know about creative design, there is evidence that engineering designers do not adhere to strictly analysis-synthesis-evaluation sequences. This evidence includes: software engineering (Guindon, 1990); large technology projects (Eckert and Stacey, 2010); and electronic circuit designers (McNeill et al., 1998). Also, engineering education research has consistently found ubiquitous creative practices (e.g., Atman et al., 2008; Turns et al., 2010). Co-evolution is the norm and creative engineers start young, which is no surprise, since what is a tame problem for experienced engineers may be a wicked one for novices.

## 2.2.2   GENEROSITY

Co-evolution does not cover all aspects of *developing problems* and *handling frames*. Some very important aspects involve a second key reality, *generosity*. Generous design aims to deliver as much worth as possible, beyond what user research may tell us. Worth here means delivering *benefits* that (far) outweigh *sacrifices* (costs and risks).

Possibilities for generosity arise from themes that exist in the world and inspire frame evolution. This can underpin *design wisdom* (Nelson and Stolterman, 2012), going beyond problem solving and its "focusing only on avoiding undesirable states, to focusing on intentional actions that lead to states of reality which are desirable and appropriate." While Nelson and Stolterman (2012) reserve "purpose" and "worth" as a judgement for clients and not designers, they also see the meanings and appropriation of design in the world as "intrinsic worth," which thus associates worth with products and designers as well as clients.

While design is "service on behalf of the other" (Nelson and Stolterman, 2012), design teams have a major personal stake in delivering the best service possible, which go beyond a client's brief. This personal stake is often reflected in designers' enjoyment of talking about their projects as "if talking about a favourite child" (Darke, 1979).

In his overview of Design Thinking, Cross (2011) quotes the architect Dennis Lasdun [corrected]:

*Our job is to give the client, on time and on cost, not what [s]he wants,*
*but what [s]he never dreamed [s]he wanted; and when [s]he gets it,*
*[s]he recognizes it as something [s]he wanted all the time.*

Note that such transcendence of client dreams is not grounded in user research, but in the design team's vision, empathy, and receptiveness. Cross (2011) also reviewed Kenneth Grange's 1971 redesign of the Frister and Rossmann 804 sewing machine. Asked to restyle the 804 to compete with other manufacturers' products, Grange quickly noticed that styling alone would deliver few benefits. Grange therefore developed an alternative design that went beyond re-styling to focus on improving use by adding storage, creating a better work area, and making cleaning more straightforward with less risk of needle injuries. Unlike those engineers who feel that they must design exactly to specification, Graham's *generosity* far exceeded the initial brief.

Creative designers strive to go beyond an initial brief and deliver as many benefits as possible, while also reducing costs and risks, increasing a design's *worth*. Examples of the generosity espoused by Lasdun and delivered by Grange are commonplace in the design literature. Junginger (2017) uses pictures of walking aids when communicating the value of design to government policy forums: one is grey bare metal without wheels; while the other is painted red with big wheels, a handbrake, a seat, and a shopping basket. The latter is not only better for impaired users, but also for government purchasers, since it reduces accidents, reliance on paid carers, and health problems, all of which will cost governments more than any cost difference between the crude frame and the generously equipped alternative. Similar comparisons can be made between low-cost standard spectacles, ones styled for individual tastes, and ones designed for specific activities such as sports (Cockton, 2010b). Eyesight correction is not a tame engineering design problem. People's feelings about appearance and suitability are not amenable to precise specification. Nevertheless, a short glance at any retail display of spectacle frames, from "designer" models to stylish budget versions, demonstrates that eyewear design can respond to the needs and wants of diverse populations. As a result, we rarely see spectacles or contact lenses as prostheses or assistive technologies. They are lifestyle choices, and are even worn by people with good eyesight.

In craft too, there are millennia of examples of qualities of workmanship that far exceed what would be required by function alone, even in the making of palaeolithic flint tools (Pye, 1968). Moving on millennia to the previous century, design historians such as Heskett (2017, p. 204) can pile up examples of generous design work in a single end note, e.g., the London Underground map, the Austin Mini, Mary Quant's mini skirt, and the Oxo good grips range. In each case, an existing product category is transformed by reconfiguration, reconceptualization, or both. Such design classics all begin with a designer's vision, adding worth through multiple benefits and reduced sacrifices for apparently "tamed" product categories.

Factors that early economic theories regard as exogenous become endogenous (and thus within organisations' control) in later theories considered by Heskett (2017). Design can thus contribute to competitive advantage, value creation and strategic fit, resources and capabilities, and strategic vision (Stevens and Moultrie, 2011). One case study in Stevens and Moultrie (2011) revealed design as a differentiator that added value in a variety of markets, where human-focused practices were enough to differentiate. This does not necessarily result in generous design, but may only meet customers' expectations rather than exceed them.

Heskett's (2017) *Value Creation Theory* extended Economics' *New Growth Theory* to "growth theory plus" (Weber, 2017) by *adding knowledge of users* as a factor of production, connecting knowledge of users to technology/ideas. New Growth Theory had added the latter as a factor of production to capital and labour from older theories. Austrian economic theory often includes the entrepreneur as a factor of production. Design(ers) can be included too, as another form of entrepreneur that adds generosity to knowledge of users.

An open framing of problems in design practice, and its associated competences, which is not restricted to knowledge of users, extends economic inputs beyond "labour" to human capital, skills, and knowledge. Knowledge management becomes crucial for innovation. Takeuchi and Nonaka's (1986) analysis of Japanese consumer product innovation built on and fed into the second author's expertise as a pioneer of knowledge management research and practice.

Dorst's focus on problem framing does not explicitly identify designers' generosity as a key factor in radical innovation, nor does he explicitly identify knowledge of users, as Heskett did. His lessons from design are at a higher level of abstraction (e.g., frame, theme, development, discourse) than specific design practices. Nevertheless, a problem framing that is radically innovative brings goals for design purpose that originate from designers' vision and passion as much as from implications of user research. Inspirations for design can achieve more than implications for design.

## 2.2.3    REFLECTIVE COMMUNAL CONVERSATIONS VIA THE MATERIALS OF A DESIGN SITUATION

Dorst's fifth lesson, fostering a discourse, is an example of the third key reality of creative practice, extending "conversation with the materials of a design situation" to include social deliberation *via* these materials. Given the multidisciplinary design teams involved in contemporary commercial, public, and third-sector innovation, discussions on the current state of design work and its forward direction are vital. Such discussions drive co-evolution.

Themes are conceptual "materials of a design situation" and as such, when they do connect with problem or solution spaces, it may well be through Schön's (1992) *backtalk* (Dorst does not speculate thus, but only notes designers' lack of deliberate or systematic ways to deal with themes). As with co-evolution, backtalk involves a range of practices and expertise. *Judgement* is vital here. Petroski (1994) stresses the self-critical faculty of the designer: "the first and most indispensable design tool is judgement." Nelson and Stolterman (2012) propose ten forms of judgement in design.

There are inevitably gaps in the backtalk of design materials to designers. Designers must thus bring their own vision and direction to conversations with both materials and colleagues. They must also bring their judgement. Conversation with the materials of a design situation are not always playful chit chat, but can involve important ethical deliberations that a linear engineering design process could freeze out before requirements specification. This is now especially important in the context of increased use of artificial intelligence and data mining from online interactions (Woodruff, 2019). When and where design decisions with potential adverse consequences have low or no reversibility, the precautionary principle (Arrow and Fischer, 1974) may have to apply.

### 2.2.4    THREE INTIMATELY CONNECTED REALITIES

The three key realities of creative design practice are intimately connected. They cannot be rigidly separated. Backtalk conversations and generosity can be understood as two key practices that can drive co-evolution, supported by judgement, expertise, and other resources. While it is possible to have co-evolution without generosity, it needs conversations with materials.

Design management must respect the realities of creative design work. Problem and solution spaces must *co-evolve* concurrently. A team's "reflective conversation with the materials of a design situation" (Schön, 1992) will be obstructed by sequential methodologies that limit design work within each phase, and thus silence *backtalk* between complementary activities that could happen concurrently. Lastly, it must be possible to frame problem spaces *generously*, and not be reined back prematurely to make projects (too) easy to track, manage and control.

Overall, top-down management needs to focus on coaching, mentoring, directing, and other forms of "subtle management control," another of Takeuchi and Noneka's (1986) six success factors. Design professionals who have been educated in an Arts School studio culture should have creative confidence in co-evolution, listen to backtalk, and be generous. Professionals from other design backgrounds such as engineering may be less confident, attentive, and generous, but they will still encounter co-evolution and backtalk during creative design work, even if their textbooks' methodologies reject the former and devalue the latter.

The Scrum agile methodology took its name from Takeuchi and Nonaka (1986), but overlooked four of their success factors (Cockton et al., 2016a). Design team members must be comfortable with: *built-in instability* (through lack of an upfront imposed process); *overlapping development phases* (concurrent engineering); *multi-learning* (multidisciplinary people); and *subtle management control*. Scrum only took its name, *self-organizing teams* and some *organizational transfer of learning* (through sprint and project retrospectives) from Takeuchi and Nonaka. No reasons have been given for ignoring other critical factors, which has unfortunately been to Scrum's disadvantage, gaining stability at the expense of agility, capability, and wisdom. Despite its name, Scrum imposes linear "relay" processes that obstruct co-evolution.

Radical innovation needs "multi-learned" team members who are managed subtly, can reflect on work so far, and self-direct future work to maintain an appropriate *balance* across design work. Cockton (2020b, Chapter 3) addresses balance in detail.

CloudBooks' development clearly corresponds to the first of the three key realities, as the team work concurrently on four work areas. The roadmap and current sprint may have evidence of generosity, but there was nothing in their story about that. There is some evidence of conversations between design/development (R&D) and strategy above interpretation of the roadmap, one material of their design situation. Key realities of creative design work may thus have a better fit with CloudBooks working practices than ISO9241-210. However, further improvements on the current state on the art on creative practice may be both possible and desirable.

## 2.3    WHAT ACTUALLY CO-EVOLVES?

There were no mentions of problems or solutions in the CloudBooks' story. Sales and marketing will no doubt talk of solutions in their conversations, but this occurs outside of, and mostly after, R&D. Instead they work on Strategy, User Research, Evaluation, and Development (aided by much design!).

This should be no surprise, as there is clearly a problem with problems. When a tame problem can be clearly stated in advance, there is limited need for creative work, especially when viable alternative solutions are known (which was not the case with the "solution" to the simply stated "tame" problem of Fermat's last theorem). When problems are "wicked," they are not problems as most would understand them, since it must be possible to state problems before solving them.

Rittel and Webber's (1973) use of "wicked" and "problem" is an example of being trapped by a dominant language, which is well understood by marginalised minorities. For example, in *Black Skin, White Masks* (Fanon 1967), a landmark in postcolonial thinking, Fanon notes that: "to speak a language is to take on a world, a culture" and "mastery of language affords remarkable power." Darke (1979) similarly remarked on "analysis" that "the language is deficient here." However, analysis-synthesis remains THE dominant espoused model design processes even today, regardless of who actually follows it. Gedenryd (1998) identified four fundamental principles of analysis-synthesis models, but noted that none are articulated within existing design methodology lexicons. There are *lacunae*, productive silences, and absence of presences (Derrida, 1976/1967), that divert attention from poor assumptions. Despite many problems, rational linear engineering design still holds the high ground. While agile methodologies relax on complete upfront problem analyses and requirement specification, they do not yet fully embrace some key realities of creative design practice (Cockton, 2016a). Dorst (2015) quotes Einstein: "a problem can never be solved from the context in which it arose." We need to move away from the problematic context that misrepresents how designers work. Ironically, this means moving away from problems and solutions.

As long as we continue to speak in terms of problems and solutions, we remain in the rationalist culture of idealised linear engineering design, and afford it "remarkable power" as we cover our creative skins with managerial masks. Creatives become suppressed minorities, with practices such as Dorst's (2015) themes lost in the split between problems and solutions.

Even the 1960s design process of "analysis-synthesis-evaluation" goes beyond problems and solutions. However, to normalise creative design practice, we need a new vocabulary, not just extra phases (Cockton, 2017). Rather than ask how we get to solutions, we can instead ask what choices are made to get there, bearing in mind that "a myriad of choices go into the design of any given artefact" (Gaver and Bowers, 2012). Heskett (2005) draws on his design history expertise to provide a valuable answer that encompasses this myriad of choices. For him, design outcomes result from:

*decisions … Choice implies alternatives in how ends can be achieved, for what purposes, and for whose advantage. … design is not only about initial decisions or concepts by designers, but also about how these are implemented and by what means we can evaluate their effect or benefit*

Heskett's analysis here follows a short inconsequential discussion of definitions of design. By moving away from what design "is" to "how design does," results in a clarity that escapes dictionary definitions. Gedenryd (1998) considered dictionary definitions of design with their multiple senses, e.g., a plan; a project, a reasoned purpose; an intent, a deliberate intention. Heskett's forms of design choice unpack these senses through ends (purpose, intent, intention), means (plan, project), reasons (for whose advantage), and evidence (evaluate). There are four forms here:

1. purposes, ends;

2. means (how ends can be achieved, initial decisions or concepts, how … implemented);

3. beneficiaries (for whose advantage); and

4. by what means we evaluate their effect or benefit.

We can think of these different forms of choice as being made in different design arenas, i.e.,

1. purpose;

2. artefacts (means to ends, through ownership and/or usage);

3. beneficiaries; and

4. evaluations.

Gaver and Bowers (2012) offer six examples of "concerns" that group design choices. These concerns correspond to purpose (design motivation, socio-political concerns), artefacts (functionality, aesthetics, production), and beneficiaries (people for whom intended). There is no concern in relation to evaluation, but the common HCI reference to "design and evaluation methods" can separate the latter from choices about design. However, Heskett (2005) includes evaluation, and once we take a broad view of it (e.g., to include reflection-in-action, technical feasibility, platform style, and standards conformance), we can see that we diminish design by isolating evaluation.

Only one design arena corresponds straightforwardly to a problem or solution: an artefact is a solution, but only when evaluated as delivering on purpose. Purpose may be thought of as within a problem space, but Dorst's rich analysis of frames (Section 2.1.3) above places some aspects of it in the solution space. Like Dorst's themes (Section 2.1.4), beneficiaries simply "are": they are neither within the problem nor the solution space. Indeed, for there to be a problem and a solution, they must be in both: in the former as research respondents; and in the latter as artefact users. Evaluations span both spaces, evaluating how well "solutions" solve "problems." Design arenas are more clear cut than problems and solutions, drawing on different disciplines and professional practices:

1. Product Management and Marketing

2. Software Engineering and Interaction Design

3. (and 4.) Human Sciences

Following Junginger (2017), in this book "products" will refer to goods, services, or a mix of both (as in a product-service system). Design arenas reframe design work as spanning four distinct work areas (note the similarities with CloudBooks work):

1. Product Strategy

2. R&D

3. Stakeholder Research

4. Evaluation

Table 2.1 renames the CloudBooks work areas in Table 1.1 as design arenas, as derived from Heskett's (2005) analysis of the origins of design outcomes. Its left column of provides an answer to the first group of questions at the end of Chapter 1.

*What are the main areas of design work? Can it reasonably be divided up in some way?*
*What are the alternatives to the areas in Table 1.1?*

Design arenas are worked on concurrently, which leads to the second group of questions:

*How do design work areas relate to each other? How are they connected? What sort of transitions are made as areas are connected?*

The next section begins to address this second group of questions from Chapter 1.

| Table 2.1: Two weeks of work across four design arenas by the CloudBooks team | | |
|---|---|---|
| **Design Arena** | **Week 1 Activities** | **Week 2 Activities** |
| Artefacts | Implement user stories for next sprint Prototype new capabilities from Cloudbooks road map | |
| Purpose | Answer queries from Interaction Designers about current Cloudbooks road map while framing future product strategy | |
| Evaluation | Usability work in response to customer feedback | Usability and wider UX inspection of user interface design for next sprint |
| Beneficiaries | Planned customer visits | Plan demonstrations and insight gathering procedures for upcoming trade show |

## 2.4    CREATIVE CONNECTIONS BETWEEN DESIGN ARENAS

Concurrent work in different design arenas raises a question as to how these are co ordinated. In linear engineering design, each phase is presented as systematically interfacing seamlessly with the next. The output from one phase becomes the input for the next, with nothing else needed. Dym et al. (2014) presents some of a very few examples of seamless interfaces in practice. Linear engineering design advocates can rarely demonstrate how one phase transitions to another. Does creative design have anything to offer instead, especially given the explosion of interfaces when multiple design arenas are worked on concurrently? The answer from the distinguished designer Charles Eames is yes, albeit nonchalantly:

> *Eventually everything connects—people, ideas, objects … the quality of the connections is the key to quality per se (eamesfoundation.org).*

Charles Eames has the creative confidence of designers who expect everything to connect eventually. This is echoed in more recent work on online business design (Mok, 1996), which has to:

> *…create meaningful connections among people, ideas, art, and technology, shaping the way people understand their relationships with … new products*

Nelson and Stolterman (2012) have a whole chapter on composing and connecting. Connections are often seen as "creative leaps," but analysis of design work has demystified them as bridge-building (Cross, 1997). A decade before this, Davies and Talbot (1987) interviewed UK Royal Designers for Industry (RDIs) about their work as outstanding professionals and likened the moment when designers realise that they have *the right idea* to the final adult stage of an insect, an *imago* (think of a butterfly emerging from its chrysalis). Unlike most research on creativity (which collapses diverse situated creative practices into some individual's mental "thing"), the key moment in design work is not the eureka of *having* an original idea, which comes easily to experienced designers, but the moment of suddenly and effortlessly *realising* that one is the *final* idea. While there may moments of illumination and verification, ideation and realisation can be separated by long time intervals. For Goldschmidt (2014), solidification of a major idea or combination of ideas is the most critical thing in design work. Her research is based on detailed studies of design work, and thus complements and validates Davies and Talbot's interview-based research. Despite all this, contemporary design research can still write about "inexplicable imaginative leaps" (Gaver and Bowers, 2012). For Darke (1979), it "seems normal for there to be a 'rationality gap'" and for Dorst (2015) "the ideation of a new frame is largely a creative leap." No study of design practice has shown that creative leaps do not exist, but many design moves are reasoned, some much more than others.

Davies and Talbot (1987) provides a rich description of *imago* moments. It brings together positions on design work across decades of professional and research sources. People and things come together at favourable junctures in wholeness and unity into a unique harmonious synthesis, echoing the Pragmatist philosopher Peirce's (1878) "continuity of consciousness" where nothing is experienced or understood in physical or temporal isolation. Kolko (2015) also focuses on synthesis rather than ideation as the core competence in design work. The architect and designer Alvar Aalto frequently referred to harmony as a goal (Stewart, 2017). In an imago, Eames' connections get made, and Cross' bridges get built, whether not they are rational, controllable, or manageable. Previously unrelated and apparently disparate reference frames become related and integrated. Before this happens, RDIs experienced their work as being in "this terrible porridge" and "developing a compost heap" out of which "an idea eventually grows" (Davies and Talbot, 1987).

Davies and Talbot extend these positions (on what designers do) with research on how RDIs experienced an imago. RDIs reported that the emergence of an imago was accompanied by deeply felt positive ecstatic pleasure, a loss of anguish, and certainty about the rightness of the idea, which they nevertheless continue to refine and test and may still reject. They look at similarities between imago experiences and spiritual ones such as "being the knowing." Such spiritual experiences could be a better model for design practice than rational systematic ideals. Gedenryd (1998) notes a dictionary's fifth sense of design: "to create or execute in an artistic or highly skilled manner." However, art and skill are not enough: creative journeys involve much more of our human condition.

As with Dorst's frames and themes, an imago is arrived at intuitively and can be ephemeral and elusive, difficult or even impossible to analyse, with its reasons or process origins often hard to articulate rationally. The RDIs were not always working on their own, but needed to win others over, but where an imago could be rationalised, others may not find this acceptable.

Contemporary multidisciplinary design teams need to find approaches and resources that make integration explicit in ways that let reasons and process origins be articulated rationally and acceptably. Darke's (1979) classic study of architects is early evidence of how some designers can recall their processes well (complementing published accounts by elite architects such as Spence, Utzon, and Lasdun), although others "found it difficult to describe a non-verbal process in words." The key skill here maybe being able to treat design work as *storytelling* (Erickson, 1996) and thus tell the *story* of how the right idea was found, rather than the *rationale* for it. The contrast here between rationality and storytelling is well established by Bruner's (1985) contrast of a *paradigmatic* (or logico-scientific) mode of thought with a *narrative* one.

Integration in multidisciplinary design teams is less likely to result from the anguished arrival of Davies and Talbot's imago and more from conscious collaborative deliberative reflection. More recent work on innovation writes of "alignment around big ideas" (Joost et al., 2010). Such deliberative alignment needs to be readily open to relevant opportunities with good prospects. This should ease acceptable rationalisation, perhaps as a joint narrative of how key design moves were made and then gathered into a coherent whole. Cockton (2020b, Chapter 4) addresses such integration in detail.

## 2.5    UNDERSTANDINGS OF CREATIVE DESIGN WORK IN HCI RESEARCH

This chapter began with consideration of the recently updated HCD standard, which gives the impression that HCI work takes no realities of creative design work into account. This has become less true recently. Early HCI research had an engineering design focus.

Histories of HCI research are often organised around three disciplinary waves: cognitive, social, and richly human. The first cognitive wave was almost completely aligned with engineering values (e.g., Card et al., 1983; Gould and Lewis, 1985), hence "usability engineering is … grounded in classical engineering" (Good et al., 1986). This first wave "may have seemed a bit brash": "too much attention was paid to applying psychology and too little understanding what it was that psychology was being applied to" (Carroll, 1990). A second social wave was humbler with participatory approaches and more creative design practices. The current richly human third wave has broadened HCI's scope beyond work to leisure to include affective experience, values, and creative design-led approaches.

Unsurprisingly, HCI's understandings of creative design practices have most improved during the current third wave. However, some key HCI researchers were studying creative design well before the first HCI conferences (e.g., Thomas and Carroll, 1979). Some of this research was framed as cognitive science rather than HCI research in support of Interaction Design practice. For example, Jeffries et al. (1981) chose a tame problem for a deliberately "straightforward" experimental task, but even this revealed that "textbook knowledge is not sufficient."

To present a fair position on improving understandings of creative design work in HCI, we consider three highly cited papers (averaging over 300 citations each by 2019) that were published in the long transition from second to third wave HCI. Later papers strongly reference earlier ones, and all draw on the first edition of Nelson and Stolterman (2012). There are many other design focused HCI papers from this period that could be considered, but the three chosen provide a coherent interesting focus for the growth of design awareness in HCI.

Löwgren (1995), in the first ACM Designing Interactive Systems conference, is a good publication to consider first. It is essentially a practice as research paper, grounded in two projects that he worked on, and moving from practice to research via retrospective critical reflection on his practice. He was motivated by "the remarkably bad fit between how the process is described in normative process models and methodologies, and how it is performed in practice." He references initial HCI research on design practices during the transition from first to second wave (either side of 1990), and also work from the first quarter century of research into design. What HCI researchers wrote did not match how he designed, so he looked to mainstream design research for better understandings.

As above, Löwgren contrasted perspectives and views from *creative design* and *engineering design*:

> *Engineering design assumes that the "problem" to be solved is comprehensively and precisely described, preferably in the form of a requirement specification. The mission of engineering design is to find a solution to the problem.*

> *Creative design work is seen as a tight interplay between problem setting and problem solving. … the design space is explored through the creation of many parallel ideas and concepts. The given assumptions regarding the problem are questioned on all levels. Creative design work is inherently unpredictable.*

By referencing similar sources as Section 2.2, Löwgren reached similar conclusions. However, he does not keep perspectives and views separate, often because his sources do not. Two research themes from one source have an engineering bias: normative models for the design process; analysis of design problems, their distinctiveness and how they should be solved. The others are more neutral: nature of design work in practice and reflections on design work.

His case studies differ: in one, the design team have "high-tempered and emotional debates, oriented towards determining the 'best' alternative"; in the other, they understand

> *…that the differences between the concepts reflected differences in ideas about the users' future work. A very lively and fruitful discussion followed, which resulted in (1) design being*

*recognized by the project manager as an explorative activity, and (2) the articulation of a*
*strategy for the product from the users' perspective.*

Löwgren's writing mixes creative and engineering perspectives. The language of one can override the other. Thus, the three steps of his adopted process (conceptual, constitutive, consolidatory) are "not sequential in time" (creative overrides engineering), but an engineering *generate and test* approach matches design visions to solution formats alongside creative *searches* that leverage expertise and judgement. This reinforces the argument in Section 2.3 that language entrenches engineering design values and practices even when they are inappropriate: "process model," "problem setting," and "problem solving" are not neutral terms, but "design work" is. Löwgren's adopted process came from "design methodology," a continuation of research *for* design work from the 1960s and 1970s, which continued to prefer sequential process concepts. Three years after Löwgren's paper, Gedenryd (1998) noted the fragmented nature of insights from research *into* design and the need to relate them to an overarching bigger picture (as in Section 2.2). Without a bigger picture to make sense of design work, engineering design concepts would continue to dominate as there was no "real theoretical alternative to them" (Gedenryd, 1998).

Mixed vocabularies expose the transitional state of design research halfway through Dorst's 50 years. Löwgren (1995) may see a "remarkably bad fit," but still used the language that spawns that, making a good fit hard to describe. Löwgren takes both "problem setting" and "problem solving" from Schön (1983), compounding Rittel and Webber's (1973) failure to drop that problematic word (Section 2.3). Even within the last decade in HCI, research at the leading edge of creative design such as (Gaver, 2011) continues to mix appropriate terms such as *design proposals, extrapolate, speculate, approaches*, and *array of resources* with legacy vocabulary such as *problem, solution, method, transform*, and *generate* from earlier design methodology.

Two thirds of the way through Dorst's (2015) half century of research into creative design, Fallman (2003) was better equipped for keeping creative and engineering perspectives separate, which he respectively referred to as *romantic* and *conservative* accounts of design. He too noted that in HCI "issues of design have not received proper attention," with "the design process ... often obliterated from research." Fallman makes good use of Löwgren (1995), but draws more directly on mainstream design research, preferring original sources to secondary accounts of design research history, but he only cites two sources by one author for his romantic account. Other possible sources often have a craft focus, but these do relate designers' responsibilities to pragmatic contexts (e.g., Pye, 1978). Nelson and Stolterman (2012) also relate carefulness in craft to a "design's worth."

Fallman's third account is also *pragmatic* and draws extensively on Schön, and thus a key reality (Section 2.2.3). This situated account of design work elaborates extensively on Jeffries et al.'s (1981) discovery that "text book knowledge is not sufficient." Fallman's contrasting three accounts of design are followed by an analysis of the relationship between design and research, where a consideration of iteration relates Schön's conversations to the unfolding of problem setting/solving.

Neither Löwgren and Fallman see any current approach to design as either perfect or completely inadequate. Fallman sees his three accounts of design as complementary. None should be completely discarded. Löwgren argues for an "appealing compromise," based on shifts of designer initiative and independence between the conceptual, constitutive, and consolidatory steps of his adopted process. The conceptual step is guided by the designer's vision, and the consolidatory step by their professional expertise, but stakeholders "can play a more active role" in the constitutive step. This middle step's contextualisation of a design may force a complete rethink. Interestingly, Löwgren associates Lasdun's generosity above (Section 2.2.2) with "the solitary genius of truly creative and inventive design," associating Lasdun with Fallman's romantic account of design.

Three quarters of the way through Dorst's half century, Wolf et al. (2006) drew on both Löwgren (1995) and Fallman (2003), but the only new design research reference is their first, which is interestingly the introduction to a practice-based research conference. This brings a research *through* design perspective (Frayling, 1993). Löwgren's critical constructive reflection on his practice drew largely on the research *into* design literature. As a *practice as research paper*, there was limited if any research rigour in the collaborative practice that Löwgren reflected critically on. The research elements were retrospectively recovered as examples of the value of creative practice in software design. In contrast, Wolf et al. (2006) write of their *practice-based research*, which used methodologies that had developed substantially since 1995. They focus on demonstrating the rigour *present* in their design research practice through research elements that were there from the outset.

A research *through* design approach, and the first author's design education in multiple craft spaces, makes Wolf et al. (2006) very different paper to Löwgren (1995) and Fallman (2003). Fallman's is primarily analytical and critical, while Löwgren's revisits two case studies through the lens of early 1990s design methodology. Wolf et al. visualise the theoretical bases of their research practice. Theirs is primarily a research *through* design paper, whereas Löwgren's is primarily a research *for* design paper (through proposing a more creatively appropriate process model). Fallman's is primarily a research *into* design paper. Löwgren and Wolf et al. do have research into design elements. They are primarily based on secondary sources in Löwgren, whereas Wolf et al. is primarily based on the primary source of their documented design research practice.

Wolf et al.'s (2006) opening paragraph confidently takes a stronger position than Löwgren and Fallman "that typical HCI usage of design is at best limiting and at worst flawed." The best usage is limiting because "as many have noted, creative design is better suited for wicked problems … [but] there is a tendency to present [work] only in its final state, losing the complexity of the creative design … process and effectively treating wicked problems as if they were tame." Papers present and discuss "problems in a way that is contrary to the nature of design," e.g., details of iteration, and the creative practices that drive it, can be absented when reporting research.

Wolf et al. argue for the rigour of their *design praxis* based on: a nonlinear process (i.e., co-evolution); design judgement (Nelson and Stolterman, 2012); making artefacts; and design critique. They also draw attention to an embracing design culture where technical language, interpretation, communication, collaboration, introspection (i.e., reflection), and deliberation combine in practice to produce designs that converge and cohere with "the myriad requirements to which they must be responsive" (i.e., through creatively connecting, Section 2.4). They apply six of Nelson and Stolterman's (2012) ten forms of design judgement to a visual representation of their design praxis for the Rendezvous system, which prevents the obliteration of the design process in descriptions of research that they and Fallman object to. This is one of the first substantial visualisations of creative practice in HCI. Its basis for rigour is explored further in Chapter 5.

Wolf et al. argue for the importance of language from creative design, as used in "critiques," but as with Löwgren, their writing can be compromised by use of engineering terms such as "process" and a compliant visual language that linearises the nonlinear. They are not alone here.

Contemporary linear box and arrow diagrams of the "Design Thinking Process" carry caveats that the process isn't really linear. This long-standing practice will may be almost 60 years old soon, as Archer (1963/4) noted for his 9-phase, 229-step *Systematic Method for Designers*: "In practice, the stages are overlapping and often confused, with frequent returns to early stages when difficulties are encountered and encountered and obscurities found." Creative design cannot be accurately communicated using inappropriate written and visual language from unsympathetic disciplines.

In over a dozen years since the last of the three focus papers above, design research has greatly strengthened its position within HCI. The ACM CHI conference has had a Design subcommittee for papers since 2008. The Research through Design conference series was established in 2011 (first conference RTD 2013, www.researchthroughdesign.org). This has much improved the environment for *research through design* work, but there has been less progress in HCI support for research *into* or *for* creative design. Much, if not most, of the design work presented at CHI and related conferences is not submitted to specialist creative design committees or venues. Outside of a few creative design enclaves, conservative accounts of design still predominate. Creative design research now has a good beachhead in HCI, but the hinterland is not yet friendly territory. Creative design research will not be fully empowered to develop strong appropriate understandings of it in an HCI that remains overly detached from mainstream design research, as well as too attached to engineering design traditions through continued inappropriate use of its language and practices.

None of the three papers propose to oust engineering design from HCI, but to complement it appropriately. A flexible mix of conservative, romantic, and pragmatic accounts of design is needed. Wolf et al. (2006) "do not put creative design above engineering design," but nor must engineering design be put above creative design. Poor understandings of creative *and* actual engineering design prevent a flexible mix. Gaver and Bowers (2012) thus argue for helping other disciplines "to appreciate how [creative] design works" while simultaneously bridging to them.

## 2.6    CHAPTER SUMMARY

Almost 50 years of research across the design spectrum (e.g., software and electronics as well as graphics and architecture) is consistently clear that, tame problems aside, creative designers do not:

1. plan or otherwise adopt a fixed process in advance and stick to a predetermined balance, with the outputs of one phase becoming the input to the next: integration is not achieved via generation, translation, or other quasi-mathematical mappings between phases;

2. work on one phase only at a time, but evolve various aspects of design in parallel: design arenas co evolve, with balance and integration partially managed via reflection; or

3. close early on a problem definition and stick to it: problem situations are framed in ways that let designers be generous and deliver worth beyond any requirements or brief.

The reasons for this are very well understood as a result of decades of research. However, those without insider knowledge as creative designers can miss "the most interesting points" (Darke, 1979), not only as researchers, but as readers. For Löwgren (2013), "a designer has unique access to the original design intentions, the history of how the design space was explored, how the process related to previous work, how different treatments were assessed, what data came out of empirical evaluations, and so on." Documentation of design processes, especially within research, has been improving, but Gaver (2011) still compares reading and viewing such documentation as "a conversation among old friends [that] may be hard for an outside to comprehend." We still need to work to help project partners and other audiences understand creative design work.

Insiders' sympathetic studies of creative design reveal realities. Three key ones are of most interest.

1. *Co-evolution* of design arenas (rather than problems and solutions), which bring challenges with balance and integration that are addressed by a wide range of creative responses. There is a good understanding of this in some HCI research. Its main implications are for the (process) structure of design work and how to track it (Chapters 4 and 5).

2. *Generous* framings of problem situations and preferred solutions (Cross, 2011; Dorst, 2015). There is little, if any, understanding of such romantic gifts in HCI research. We use reflective axiological design resources to communicate what is needed here (Book 2, Cockton 2020b, Chapter 2).

3. Schön's (1992) "reflective conversation with the materials of a design situation" within a broader social discourse (Dorst, 2015). Knowing emerges within immersive design activities from "backtalk," both during (reflection in action) and between activities (reflection on action). Backtalk can both drive forward work within specific design arenas and also support their integration. This is well understood in some HCI research. Its main implications are for supporting deliberative reflective use of design resources (Cockton, 2020b, Chapters 2, 3, and 4).

However, universal abstract process models, with fixed sequences of homogeneous development activities, remain very popular, even in supposedly designerly practices of Design Thinking (Waloszek, 2012) and Design Sprints (Knapp et al., 2016). Decades of well-informed papers on the realities of design practice have not overcome the conservative account of design. Objectively countering the conservative account with the realities of creative design has been ineffective for half a century now, so the next chapter takes a more creative approach and confronts conservative values via fiction. While this may be innovative within HCI, it is a well-established practice elsewhere, e.g., *Harvard Business Review* Cases, which are "fictional, present common managerial dilemmas and offer concrete solutions from experts" (Wetlaufer, 1997).

Fiction may be better placed to expose absurdities and delusions. The content of the next chapter is not all imaginary however. No character's position has been made up. Much is fictionalised material from 30 years of teaching, research, and work in, with, and for software companies and digital agencies. Positions that object to well-established results from research into design are often motivated by technical management priorities that ignore the needs of creative practice. Unsurprisingly, these rarely come from industry, but instead from textbooks, standards and reviews of research papers, even for venues that are design oriented. These are all outsiders' positions.

Fictionalised accounts are not standard practice in technical writing, but decades of compliant writing have achieved little. Reason and evidence are highly valued by conservative accounts unless they reveal misconceptions and inaccuracies. It is thus appropriate to use creative writing to defend creative practice and to expose the failings of its oppressors. Readers, I wrote some.

CHAPTER 3

# We Need to Talk About Process: A Design Practice Research Fiction

The design practice research fiction that follows interrogates advocates of engineering design models that are *rational*, *linear*, and *idealised* (Parnas and Clements, 1986), which will be abbreviated to RILED: Rational Idealised Linear Engineering Design. Dorst (2017) identifies the primary motive for RILED models as control, but this is not "subtle management control" in Takeuchi and Nonaka's (1986) sense. At its extreme, in Stage-Gate models, such control undermines creative innovation (Christensen and Kaufman, 2008). However, RILED's advocates prioritise values over evidence. Five decades of argument and evidence from design research have failed to change RILED claims, so one creative response is to use fiction, as increasingly used in design research and practice. As befits creative work, humour helps out. This lets us confront emotion with emotion.

*Design Fiction* became a focus in design research around 2010 (Blythe and Encinas, 2016). Design fictions explore artefact futures, i.e., imagined uses and impacts of imagined new technologies and applications. They aim to explore issues and promote debate. Chapter 1 began with a novel design *practice* fiction about an imagined artefact (Cloudbooks) and the imagined work to develop it. This chapter adds a further novel form, a design *practice research* fiction, which involves imagined designers and researchers taking positions on the nature of design best practice. To fulfil research requirements, they must include citations (Cockton, 2057), unlike other forms of design fiction.

A design practice research fiction is used below to create a distance that may hopefully prompt readers with engineering or (scientific) management backgrounds to reflect on their beliefs. Gaver (2011) relates fictional voices to a "critical remove," inspired by the fictitious inventors of the artist Kaborov. Equally, such voices can hopefully inspire readers with creative design backgrounds to challenge RILED's advocates and guide them towards realistic positions.

I have been using a range of literary devices for over a decade to cut through the complacency of uncritical advocates of RILED practice: drama (Cockton, 2008d), parody (Cockton, 2012a, 2012b), and humanities influenced critical essays (Cockton 2008b, 2009a, 2013c, 2017). Had logical positivism succeeded, there would be no need to break away from conservative technical writing practices. Were there universally accepted public criteria for sound arguments and adequate evidence, I would prefer those over other forms of persuasion. However, the necessary criteria do not yet exist. If they did, there would be a clear way to force concessions. Until then, RILED advocates can persist with flimsy arguments and meagre evidence.

Eight named characters in the design practice research fiction give voice to positions and expertise that are rarely encountered in mainstream HCI: product managers; large engineering projects; craft practices; creative confidence; design work environments; the economic value of design work; and young hybrid creative professionals with multiple design and research competences. Unnamed ultra conservatives also voice strong positions on engineering design that rarely appear in writing, creating telling lacunae in the RILED lexicon that masks their existence (Gedenryd, 1998). In addition to these gaps, technical writing standards exclude strongly felt statements of personal experience. RILED has us surrounded! We may have to shoot our way out!

## 3.1    A SIX-ACT FICTION

Our design practice research fiction is in seven acts. It starts in 2020 with an international panel to review the adequacy of current engineering design textbooks, (de facto) process standards and design curricula. Promising recent developments such as the U.S. *Consortium to Promote Reflection in Engineering Education* (CPREE—cpree.uw.edu) and the UK *New Model in Technology and Education* (NMiTE—nmite.ac.uk) would seed worldwide improvement of graduates' innovation competences.

The panel comprises well-read pragmatic researchers who seek plausible arguments supported by fair evidence, and not posturing or grandstanding about "Design Science" (have no "design scientists" read about the demise of logical positivism?). They accept that different designers will do things differently and are more concerned with excellent work from the best designers than poor work from the worst. In a positivist world, all designs in response to a well-formed brief would be the same, because logic and evidence would converge to one replicable solution. The panel thus has no normative agenda for how design work must be conducted (but they are very keen on design arenas derived from Heskett's writing). They have good knowledge across widely ranging professional practices about research into creative design. They have long suffered colleagues' disciplinary agendas that insist on telling creative designers how to work. Over their careers, they have been repeatedly inundated by tsunamis of false assumptions. Despite that, they remain open-minded and prefer asking to judging. They would be a great asset at Design School critique sessions.

The panel want a fair inquiry, which wouldn't be easy given existing entrenched positions. They'd like to wipe the slate clear, and one wondered if the philosopher Rawl's (1971) *veil of ignorance* would help. The panel weren't sure until a quick web search gave them an educationalist's version (Maxcy, 2002, p. 93) that they could quickly modify for their purpose:

> *We have set the task of faithfully developing a radical new approach to design. We will minimize but not eliminate all personal biases and prejudices.*
> *We will imagine ourselves in a world with no design methodologies, behind a veil of ignorance, behind which we know nothing of ourselves and our aptitudes.*

*We know nothing of our education, achievements, or professional values.*
*Behind this veil, we are all reasonable and autonomous (epistemologically and axiologically*
*equal). We know that in the "real world," there will be wide variety in the disciplinary dis-*
*tribution of values and practices, and that differences of education and achievements mark*
*out groups of people.*

"Well, that's us off to very good start" said the panel chair, "but perhaps we should introduce ourselves now. I'm Claudia Schmidt. I study large advanced engineering projects." "I'm Johan Smed. I study creative uses of digital technologies." "I'm Daniela Fabbri. I study the roles of materials in design work." "I'm Aram Darbinyan. I study creative confidence." "I'm Soyoung Ju. I study design work environments." "I'm Mohan Corea, I study the economic value of design work." "Welcome everyone, and thank you all very much for joining this panel" said Claudia.

### 3.1.1    ACT 1: JOHAN DRAWS FOR MOHAN

Our panel begin with a team building exercise. Johan shares the now famous work of the award-winning CloudBook's team. He asks if there are other ways to look at it. "There seem to be no stages or distinguishable episodes" notes Claudia. "That's because it masks the details of current, next and future releases" says Mohan, "field visits relate to the current version, design and development work to the next release, and strategy to future releases after that. Evaluation spans all releases." Johan quickly fills out Table 3.1 and says "this isn't going to be easy, I mean, trying to model concurrent work across multiple releases as a single uniform design process. It's a *programme*, not a project."

Table 3.1: The past, present, and future of work in design arenas

| Design Arena | Current version | Next Release | Future releases |
|---|---|---|---|
| Artefacts | Finished and in use | Design-led work, other interaction design, and coding for next release | Prototyping |
| Purpose | Finished (just?) before implementation of current version | Answering questions from interaction designers about how next release fits into the CloudBooks roadmap | Competitor and trend analysis, replacement product analysis, product strategy development |
| Evaluation | Participant panel management | Next release testing and inspection | Competitor product testing, prototype testing and inspection, participant panel recruitment |
| Beneficiaries | Customer visits to users of current release | | Plan demonstration and insight gathering for upcoming trade show |

Soyoung asks "is it fair?" All agree that it is fair in the sense of being consistent with the evidence before them, but they don't have much detail to work from. Even so, they've formed an initial shared understanding of design arenas, stages, episodes, release schedules, and roadmaps. They need to explore complementary understandings of design work, so they plan a focus group.

### 3.1.2    ACT 2: BRING ME MY ARROWS OF DESIRE

The panel have been given analyses of online positions on design methodology by their big data team, who have scraped the web for views on CPREE in the U.S. and NMiTE in the UK. Sentiment analysis revealed a range of responses, from very positive to very negative. There were too many to cover in a single focus group, so a sample was picked at random and the online presence of each was analysed for their positions on engineering design. Some of their online content included models of design processes, such as Figure 3.1. There were a very wide range of positions in their comments that made a balanced focus group unworkable, so the panel decided to run an "out of focus" group of the most negative respondents. This would let them understand conservative positions on design.

When the Negatively Out Of Focus (NOOF) group had gathered online, they were greeted and thanked for helping. Those gathered thanked the panel in return, as they were all very keen to ensure that the review is well informed with the best that engineering design has to offer. Figure 3.1 was shared via the video conferencing system, as the panel had prepared questions on it.

1. How much of the process is spent on problems and how much on solutions?

2. There is a fixed order of boxes in the diagram. Why is this?

3. What happens as you move from one phase to the next? How do phases interface? How do outputs from one phase function as inputs to the next?

4. What is the nature of the verification and validation feedback? Is any iteration involved, and if so what happens?

The questions were asked in turn. The answer to the first question was that there was one problem box and four solution ones, but less than 20% of the time should be spent on the problem. "Why?" asked Daniela. "Because the client should be clear about their problem, so once it's really clear, you can start thinking about the main needs and constraints" was the reply. "But what if the problem is problematic?" asked Mohan. "It shouldn't be" was the reply. "I'm surprised" said Aram, who looked for a definition of problem with his smartphone. "Merriam-Webster will do, gotta love their search engine optimisation. OK, so there are two groups of senses. One is problematic things such as intricate unsettled questions, a source of perplexity, distress, or vexation, or something difficult to understand or accept. The other sense is more straightforward, so if problematic problems aren't welcome, then how about a question that needs solving?" "No," said the NOOF group in unison. One continued "questions get answered, problems get solved." "All that's left then," Mohan responded "is a proposition in physics or mathematics stating something to be done." "That's it," said the NOOF group in unison, "just like we had in school." "You mean on a problem sheet provided by a tutor who has checked that you can do it?" asked Soyoung. "Of course," said the NOOF group in unison.

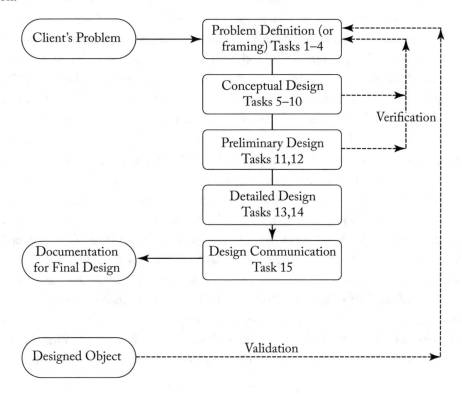

Figure 3.1: Engineering design process (Dym and Little, 2009).

"That's very interesting," said Claudia, "so does that help with our second question on why there is a fixed order?" "Well you clearly can't solve a problem until you know what it is," was the reply "and once you do you work from an outline solution and refine it to a detailed one." "OK," said Claudia, "so how do you progress between phases? Can you give examples of dependencies, interfaces and flows?" The responses were very abstract. Nothing concrete was communicated: no examples were offered. The panel did not expect much now as an answer to the last question. They were right. The answer given was simply "well, it's either verified or it's not, and if it's not it must get fixed."

These short vague answers did not seem to bother the NOOF group. They had answered all the questions, which were very abstract and philosophical. If they'd been asked well-specified concrete questions they could have given much better answers. They were all very knowledgeable, but their knowledge was about the useful practical knowledge that got things done. They liked Figure 3.1, however, which originated from highly respected engineering design educators. "There are far worse models out there," said one, "that have not been kept as simple as this one." "We agree," replied Aram "that's why we chose it as a focus for our first session. It stood out from others."

With 40 minutes of the hour video conference left, the panel revisited the answers, asking first what logical dependencies were. "They're the dependencies that mean that phases must come after each other," was the answer. "But what are these dependencies?" Claudia asked. "Ones that mean you can't start a phase until you've finished all the earlier ones," was the reply. "Oh we see," said Daniela (who didn't). She tried another approach to teasing out some concrete content: "so that's why there are arrows between boxes?" "Exactly!" replied the NOOF group in unison.

Daniela continued: "So what does an arrow show? What goes in at its start and what comes out at its end?" One of NOOF group replied that nothing actually goes in or comes out, the arrow just jumps from the end of one phase to the start of another. Daniela asked: "so why not just miss out the arrows and stack the phases or abut them side by side? The process order must be obviously implied by those well understood logical dependencies? You know, like in the Open Systems Interconnection model for networked communication?" An NOOF engineer came straight back: "That's an abstract architectural model, not a process model. Process models always have arrows." "But do the arrows do anything?" asked Soyoung. "No!" the NOOF group replied in unison.

There was no point in revisiting the questions again, so Mohan added a new one that interested him: "How are the people being designed for involved in this process? What do they do in each phase?" How the NOOF group laughed! One explained why they thought that this was funny.

*We are all engineers who only work on well-specified hard problems. We don't do any soft stuff involving people because that's too fuzzy. We prefer calculations. We let others do that. I think it's human-centred design or something like that.*

The panel thanked the NOOF group for their participation. After the video conference they asked their big data team to collect and analyse a new corpus of data about HCD. They then returned to writing up their first session.

The pain of writing up the session was eased by their knowledge that where logic was unsurprisingly of limited help, there was extensive empirical evidence as to what actually happens in design work (mostly outwith the bounds of logic). Hopefully, the HCD group in the next session could bring more concrete wisdom to the inquiry.

"So is this veil of ignorance useful?" asked Claudia. "There must be no arrows behind it," joked Daniela, "so I'm staying behind it!" "Write that in our recommendations," added Aram, "no arrows!"

### 3.1.3    ACT 3: ASK A STANDARDS QUESTION, GET A STANDARD ANSWER

The big data team quickly found the ISO 9241-210 standard (Figure 3.2) and decided to save some time and just invite online advocates of the standard. Sites such as uxqb.org indicated that there were thousands of certified professionals who could explain how the standard works. Analysis of online content indicated a range of detail and enthusiasm. The most knowledgeable and enthusiastic advocates of ISO standard HCD were thus invited to a second "well in focus" group.

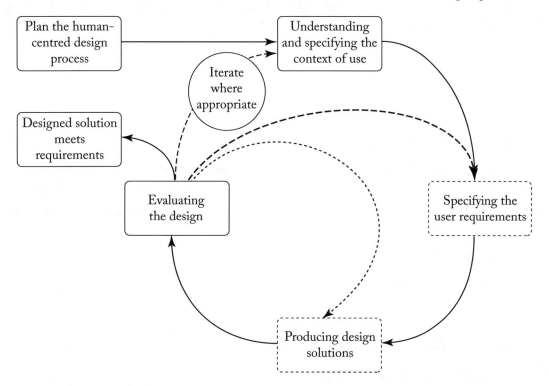

Figure 3.2: HCD Process for ISO 9241-210 (dotted iteration was in predecessor ISO13407 standard, dashed iterations are new to 9241-210, arrow annotations from 2019 revision not shown, two boxes dashed by Soyoung).

The video conference software was used to share Figures 3.1 and 3.2. When all had gathered online, they were greeted and thanked. The HCD group thanked the panel back, as they were all very keen to ensure that the review was well informed with good knowledge of the best HCD process standard.

The panel asked their NOOF questions indirectly by asking the HCD group to compare Figures 3.1 and 3.2, focusing on where problems were addressed, the need for a fixed order, and the interfaces between phases, including iterative feedback. The consensus was that problems were either addressed in the first phase or two, depending on how what form user requirements took. With no requirements in Figure 3.1 it was hard to compare the two process models from their diagrams.

The panel decided that they needed to understand Figure 3.1 and contacted their big data lead, Kirsty McGowan, to see if she had information on what the tasks were. "Now you ask," Kirsty said, "we'd been meaning to tell you … ." It turned out that much web content made use of Figure 3.1, which was from a third edition, but that had been superseded by a fourth (Dym et al., 2014). "However" Kirsty continued, "the newer version is more complicated, but does show all tasks, i.e.,

1. revise client's problem statement;

2. clarify objectives;

3. identify constraints; and

4. establish principal functions.

There's a mistake in the diagram," said Kirsty, "but the text after it makes it clear. The outputs from this first phase (*Problem Definition: Detailing Customer Requirements* in 4th ed.) are the inputs to the next (*Conceptual Design: Translating Customer Requirements into Engineering Specifications*) are:

1. customer requirements;

2. revised problem statement;

3. initial list of final objectives;

4. initial list of constraints; and

5. initial list of principal functions.

Also, when Soyoung was changing two boxes to dashed, I removed the example output annotations from the arrows in the new 2019 version of ISO9241-210. They are, respectively, from context of use, user requirements, designing, and evaluating:

1. user group profiles, as-is scenarios, personas;

2. identified user needs, desired user requirements, applicable design guidance;

3. scenarios of use, lo-fi and hi-fi prototypes; and

4. usability testing, field and user survey reports.

"Soyoung," asked Claudia, "why did you have two box outlines changed to dashed?" "Because only the top quadrant has HCD methods. The two boxes and circle correspond directly to Gould and Lewis' (1985) key principles for usability," answered Soyoung, "but I didn't know any HCD methods for the other two phases. I can see now though that there could be applicable HCD design guidance, and that scenarios of use are HCD resources. I've no idea what a design team would do with both identified user needs and desired user requirements though." "Neither have I," said Claudia.

"Well, that's useful," said Mohan "we were right with the NOOF group, and now the HCD group too, the arrows are just decoration. It would be better to just abut the phases." "Well you could," said Kirsty "but it's not like that in the 4th edition." The input and two outcomes on the left with rounded ends in Figure 3.1 had become four interfaces between phases in the fourth edition's Figure 2.1. Phase boxes are now joined to each other with two arrows with a rounded box in between. I've drawn an extract from Dym et al. (2014) and showed the single arrow version from ISO 9241-210 (Figure 3.3).

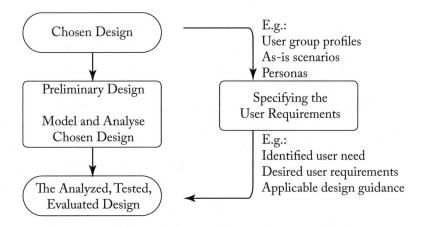

Figure 3.3: Phases, phase tasks and input and outputs.

"See, I thought there'd be something on the arrows," said Aram. "Actually, the rounded boxes are just interfaces, you could still abut them in a box joining output to input phases, as you could with the example outputs in the revised ISO9241-210 standard," said Claudia.

"Ahem," interrupted an HCD group member, "do we have anything to do here?" "Of course," replied Claudia, "it looks to me like the boxes are different in the two figures, but not wholly so. I wonder why the rounded boxes are there though?" "I've no idea," the interrupter replied, "I've never seen process diagrams with them in before." "Have any of you seen engineering design process models before?" asked Claudia. A few HCD folk half raised their hands and the rest looked puzzled. One said that ISO9241-210 was aimed at managers, so he hadn't read it.

"Dym et al. have customer requirements, but ISO9241-210 has user requirements. Who here has written user requirements?" asked Mohan. No one had. Discussion revealed that either business analysts, product managers, or software engineers wrote them, often in a core strategic group lacking HCD specialists. There was a single set of requirements with no clear way to distinguish "user requirements" from other ones. However, most of the HCD group had prepared user interface (UI) design specifications, but they wanted to be very clear that UI is not UX. "You must put that in your report!" said one of them with great gusto.

"So, if you don't write user requirements, would you mind if they weren't there?" asked Aram. "Of course we'd mind!" said an HCD expert. "Who has read any literature from the last 50 years on how creative designers work?" asked Daniela. "Why would we do that?" asked the HCD expert who'd wanted to keep analysis, synthesis and evaluation rigidly separate. "Well, has anyone?" asked Daniela (again). There were a few unconvincing nods. Soyoung then shared Kees Dorst's argument from his 2015 *Frame Innovation* book that creative designers need to work with an open problem *situation* rather than a frozen problem *definition*, since freezing the latter also freezes consideration of usage and other contexts. The HCD consensus was that iteration allows for unfreezing of both context descriptions and user requirements. Aram asked back why either should ever be frozen in the first place. "Because Scrum makes you," said one HCD expert. Perhaps agile approaches can sometimes help HCD thought Aram (but he kept that to himself).

That seemed to be a good point to end the HCD group. The panel updated the notes for their report. "Soyoung was right that there was little clear D in HCD, plus we must say that UX isn't UI!" said Johan. "Or was it that UI isn't UX?" quipped Daniela. "Getting that wrong has totally destroyed the economic value of so much Interaction Design work" Mohan grinned. Some panel members looked shocked. "Sorry, that was a joke," Mohan said, "but, when HCD experts keep complaining that they aren't valued enough, petty distractions like that don't help." "On a more serious note" said Soyoung, "we still won't want any arrows, but we do want to see some sort of interface or connections between different design activities. That newer diagram that Kirsty found clearly interfaced between phases, with outputs from one as inputs to the next. We do need some forms of connection in process models." "I agree," said Johan, "but the boxes, ovals, circles or whatever matter too. The HCD group seemed to know little about engineering or creative design. What they knew was second hand at best, as reinterpreted within HCI. Perhaps both groups would better understand creative design if they knew more about it, so to reward their participation, we could run an online seminar for them." "What a great idea," said Claudia, "we'll update our notes after your lecture, which will hopefully lead to better understandings." "My lecture?" said Johan, surprised.

### 3.1.4    ACT 4: SHOCK AND TELL

The combined groups were welcomed to a short online seminar. Johan opened with a question: "Why do we have design process models?" A recently certified HCD expert came straight back with the standard creation story for engineering project management: difficulties with military engineering during World War II necessitated structured managed approaches to R&D projects. Without such processes, projects could not be properly managed, and would not deliver on time, to specification, within budget.

Johan began with a slide on Rittel and Webber (1973) and Takeuchi and Nonaka (1986), and explained how both argued that copying NASA's rational programme and project management methodologies had constrained creative design work in ways that severely reduced its effectiveness. And of course, NASA as an organisation was severely constrained by neither deadlines nor budgets, even though getting humans onto the moon is strictly a tame problem. Johan quipped that it would be nice to get them back again too, but that wasn't part of the moon goal. No one laughed.

The combined groups were shocked and confused. They had no idea that criticisms of RILED methodologies went back almost 50 years. Their shock continued with Johan's slides on the rise and fall of the 1960s Design Methods movement, which was founded on a single belief that a single design process, revealed by "meta-design," was common to specialisms such as architecture, industrial design, architecture and planning (Darke, 1979). The groups were also unaware that two key proponents of design methods, Christopher Alexander (originally a mathematician) and John Chris Jones (originally an engineer), publicly dismissed their own analysis-synthesis models within a few years (Gedenryd, 1998), and another proponent, Hanson, reported that his method was so cumbersome that he would not use it again (Darke, 1979). Design methods failed not only as descriptions, failing to match the realities of creative design work, but also as prescriptions, failing to deliver promised results (Gedenryd, 1998). RILED and its HCI offshoot had succumbed to Mintzberg's (1994) *Fallacy of Formalisation* from business, the misconception that an imposed formal structure and process is a sensible basis for strategy formation.

Mohan chipped in that to win influence at board level in organisations, demands for overly formal processes, and rash guarantees about them may not be persuasive (and when they are, the organisation would become poor at design). Mintzberg's (1994) *Fallacy of Detachment* should also be avoided where attempts are made to base strategy solely on hard facts in objective isolation (the HCD group were at risk on that). In contrast, tacit design knowledge has strategic value as a source of inappropriable resources that the competition cannot easily copy (Heskett, 2017). Explicit support for developing such tacit resources was seen by Stevens and Moultrie (2011): where a "design culture encouraged 'personal interactions, learning by example, demonstration and participation.'"

"Thank you Mohan," said Johan, who returned to his last slides on 1990s developments. A few of the NOOF group knew of concurrent engineering (e.g., Erhorn and Stark, 1995), but not that Takeuchi and Nonaka's much earlier (1986) "scrum" paper is recognised as a very early account of it (Umemoto et al., 2004). Despite this, Jeff Sutherland and Ken Schwaber proposed *an iterative sequential* (i.e., linear relay!) Scrum methodology in a 1995 OOPSLA'95 workshop inspired by Takeuchi and Nonaka (who preferred scrum/rugby metaphors in English to the overlapping sliced fish of Japanese *sashimi*).

The main initial selling point for concurrent engineering had been reduced time to market and not its valuable enabling of creative practices (Umemoto et al., 2004). Johan used this latter position to summarise the realities of creative practice, especially co-evolution, talkbalk, and generosity.

"Any questions or comments?" asked Johan. "Yes," said an HCD expert who had found a second hand copy of Dym's (1994) first textbook, "I still see no basis for moving away from this definition":

> *Engineering design is the systematic, intelligent generation and evaluation of specifications for artefacts whose form and function achieve stated objectives and satisfy specified constraints.*

This opened the flood gates to a torrent of axiological vocabulary. The groups argued that design must also objectively achieve and satisfy, and further be complete, disciplined, evidence-based, fully informed, guaranteed, planned, reliable, rigorous, well-managed, and much more.

The panel tried to keep track of all the implied requirements for a design process. Some noted a clear value system and knew that values by their very nature cannot be inherently wrong. Positive orientations fire espousers up and generally invite support. Espousing values is relatively benign. Difficulties mostly arise when espousers try to act on them. There may be no clear way to proceed, and where there is, success may not follow. Worst of all, espousers may be unable to see that their actions lead to outcomes in conflict with espoused values. Values don't mess up, people do.

Claudia expressed doubts that anyone following a prescriptive process could ever deliver on all these espoused engineering and managerial values (Mintzberg's 1994 *Fallacy of Formalisation*). Neither group had answered any questions well, giving the panel impression that, with no clear and proven ways to deliver on such demanding values (however noble), they had only heard posturing rhetoric.

Before ending the discussion, Claudia asked if anyone wanted to say anything that had been missed. There were some passionate responses:

- "phases are indispensable—you must know what problem you are trying to solve before you can solve it—this is how process experts say they work and we should copy";

- "you cannot design without valid contextual research: you cannot begin to design anything until you know who you are designing for, how they work, and what success looks like";

- "you must demonstrate that designs work: you can't know that a design is appropriate without sufficient evidence from realistic usage in appropriate contexts"; and

- "you cannot work on different things in parallel: you must first have complete, correct and unambiguous requirements to be able to develop a valid and verifiable solution."

Claudia felt that they were going around in circles. Her response to the first comment was that they had asked for evidence of how phases worked and how they interfaced, and the best answer came via Kirsty from Dym et al. (2014) and not from either group. Claudia summed up: "You have not given good answers to our questions. To build some common ground, Johan has presented today's seminar, which was a brief introduction to the history of design methodology. None of you have engaged with any of the extensive evidence of the realities of creative design practice. Why not?" A conservative engineer quickly answered:

*Because all that research is wrong. It's all about bad design. We have no doubt at all about how good design should work, and we know that it can and does work if the right people do things the right way. We don't need evidence. We just know. It's all common sense, it's obvious. When things go wrong, it's because the proper approaches are ignored by lazy ignorant designers. We're not interested in fancy theory, psychology, ethnography or whatever. None of that subversive nonsense is worth anything. We've no time for people who rock the boat to make trouble. The only wicked problem is getting in the way of people who get things done, like us. We don't waste time on semantics and endless discussions. We're not afraid of science like you clearly are. We're not lazy. We don't mind hard work. We take pride in doing everything correctly to the highest standards.*

The panel searched around for their veil of ignorance. Could one really do away with deeply entrenched values? Would it allow the NOOF group to see that the "analysis-synthesis model is clearly wrong," with "elaborated versions" of it (Darke, 1979) as "scientist rather than a scientific way of thinking" (Dym et al., 2014 is such an elaborated model). A few software development experts reached the same conclusions as Darke a few years later. For example, Swartout and Balzer (1982) critiqued "all current software methodologies" and their adoption of "a common model that separates specification from implementation" (i.e., a form of analysis-synthesis model):

*…this model is overly naive, and does not match reality. Specification and implementation are, in fact, intimately intertwined.*

The seminar had not been as effective as the panel would have liked. They thanked everyone for attending and waited for the last member of the groups to leave. Most left the video conference uncomfortably and quickly, but the chair saw that one had stayed. She had waved at the panel straight after the last in her group left. "Can we help you?" asked Claudia. "Have you got time for a brief chat?" she replied. "I think we do," said Claudia, please remind us of your name." "I'm Marisela Rodriguez." "I'm Claudia Schreiber, please go ahead. We'll write up our notes later."

### 3.1.5    ACT 5: DANIEL YOU'RE A STAR

"I'd been quiet and listened," said Marisela "because I wasn't sure if there were others like me here. I've a creative design background, but I have my UX certification. I gained so much from learning about researching the context of use and planning evaluations. It was much more than I'd learned on my degree programme. I got really interested, so I started looking at HCI research. I soon wondered if there was 'design-oriented' HCI research. There are many creatively educated designers in digital now, so I searched for it and found this great paper by Daniel Fallman. I thought about it a lot during your lecture and the discussions. The angry responses reminded me of his *conservative* account of design, 'a scientific or engineering endeavour'. I felt that those who were angry at Johan's lecture didn't want to listen. I was happy with it, as I like Fallman's *romantic* account that 'gives prominence to the role of the designer', but I like his *pragmatic* account more. I copied it straight away into the back of my notebook. Let me read it to you, it's an account that involves":

> *…being engaged directly in a specific design situation … that … locates the design process in a world which is already crammed with people, artifacts, and practices, each with their own histories, identities, goals, and plans. Rather than science or art, under the pragmatic account design takes the form of a hermeneutic process of interpretation and creation of meaning, where designers iteratively interpret the effects of their designs on the situation at hand. It is a reflective conversation with the materials of the design situation.*

"Thank you," said Johan, "I like Fallman's paper, too. Much of it is consistent with, even identical to, mainstream research into creative design such as Davies and Talbot (1987), who observed how their *imago* always involved aspects of designers and others, but within the context of some grand scheme. In contrast with Fallman's *romantic* account, designers transcend their selves, and become *selves as others*. In contrast with Fallman's *conservative* account, designers 'make use of a Janus-faced middle ground of rationalising consciousness' where 'logical validity is sought for 'known, intuitive truths' by infusing the latter in a logical sequence. One RDI in Davies and Talbot's study referred to this as 'fine tuning … to make it a runner'. All of this is abstracted away from in a conservative account and sidelined in a romantic one."

Daniela liked how Fallman's pragmatic account draws on philosophical Pragmatism with its emphasis on integration between the individual and the environment (Rylander, 2012), which intimately links experiencing and creating. It also consistent with Quine's (1951) argument for a shift towards pragmatism, and also with Darke's (1979) "diversity and anarchy of human life." She also liked its understanding of the realities of design work. While HCI researchers has looked at creative design practices seriously in the 1990s, this was mostly as outsiders (e.g., Karat, 1991).

Johan reminded everyone that Fallman's pragmatic account is not hostile to scientific, engineering or management values, but it is realistic with respect to the situational complexities of creative design work. Nor does Fallman see the pragmatic account as superior to the conservative or romantic ones. "Oh I know," said Marisela, "and I agree. My UX certification has shown the value of the conservative account, but my experimental work on my creative degree also showed the value of the romantic account, and now my current job has shown that a pragmatic account provides a context that can bring out the best of the other accounts." "But fans of the conservative account just don't want to share the epistemic space," said Johan, "their rational value systems are very robust. They underpin many professional and academic identities. Drawing attention to these can result in conflict or personal discomfort. We should all be able to accept that all professional and academic practices are inevitably and acceptably value-laden. Some people can't though. Shame."

"These values, and their associated practices, can be very tenacious," said Daniela. "Oh, I've seen that," said Marisela, "but I think creative design is now better represented. I looked through the CHI proceedings for a few years after Fallman's paper. I found a 2011 paper by Gaver very empowering. It valued the contributions in design work from previous projects, conversations, familiar art and design work and shared cultural references. I looked at *Interactions* magazine too and I was pleased to see Gaver and Bowers (2012) value 'the situated, multidimensional, and configurational nature of design.' As a creative designer, these shared sources of ideas and insights are core to my work, but scientific HCI tends not to value these."

Marisela continued, "But you're right that rational values are very tenacious, especially as researchers make their first moves towards more creative practices. For example, I'd also found a CHI 2005 short paper by Cockton. He'd innovatively replaced ISO's first two phases with opportunity identification, also overlapped design and evaluation, and added a novel iteration phase for replanning the next cycle of development. He still had phases though, with his opportunity identification completing before evaluation could be planned. That planning in turn had to happen before design, but then the planned evaluation had to wait until design and/or development had completed. For all I know, he's still mostly thinking in terms of sequenced phases." "He's not," said Johan, "but it took him almost a decade to propose fully concurrent design arenas. It's a shame that no-one picked that up earlier, as that paper has a lot of citations. OK, it did have some concurrency, a split phase and an iteration one, but it's vital that values behind design practices are exposed."

"That sounds like a good place to stop." said Claudia, "Thank you for staying behind. Early career professionals like you can give old hands a new focus." "Yes, thank you," said Mohan, "I can't see you diving into UX vs UI nonsense." Marisela laughed, "No Way! Interaction Design's much bigger than both, and HCI is bigger still when it's not limited to usage studies. Thank you for listening to me."

"Bye," said Claudia, "now let's get back to our notes." Soyoung came straight in. For her, it had to be clear that frank discussion of design methodologies must involve axiological exposure. This is not to condemn, marginalise or undermine, but to enable genuinely transdisciplinary design practice. She knows from her research that this is regularly achieved in design practice, but never by sticking to one disciplinary axiology. She would like to get ubiquitous creative practices down on paper. Aram added that he would like to exclude partisan public positions on design advocated by those who would completely enforce a scientific basis, but could never provide personal examples of achieving this in practice. "In short, it you can't walk the walk, stop talking the talk," said Aram.

Mohan continued, "and talk talk that commands respect. While the difference between UI and UX is pointlessly debated, the full potential value of user research and evaluation is rarely being realised in design work. Both can enrich what design teams bear in mind when connecting between people and design. I mean, even politicians are human-centred these days. You can't innovate without it. But you have to deliver on human-focused work. Some advocates treat it like an unquestionable sacrament." Daniela looked shocked. "Sorry, but you know what I mean Daniela." "I do," she replied.

Johan recalled how poor interfaces between HCD process phases show up in the HCI literature, as issues over a lack of "implications for design" from user research (Dourish, 2006), and a lack of "downstream utility" for subsequent design iterations from evaluation (Law, 2006). He was not surprised that neither group had been unable to offer any evidence of how rational linear processes can be effective in practice (other than for tame problems). HCD, with its roots in human sciences, had interfaces that were more poorly defined than those in Dym et al. (2014).

"There's a lot to get down here," said Claudia, "let's start with values. The issue here is not whether it is right or wrong to want design work to be intelligent, generative, complete, disciplined, evidence-based, fully informed, guaranteed, objective, planned, reliable, repeatable, rigorous, systematic, well-managed, and other desiderata from engineering and management. Instead it is about what can be achieved, and how. And that means achieved with sufficient creative practice, which means opening up the necessary space for creative exploration."

"I agree," said Johan, "and as a start we must separate Fallman's conservative values from nonsense processes. Values are important axiological resources, but the associated process models are sheer fiction. Tame problems apart, they bring no guarantees, but well-judged application of conservative values can definitely improve concurrent creative processes."

"Absolutely!" said Aram, "just as Marisela pointed out, a pragmatic approach can balance making room for the realities of creative design work on the one hand, with taking every opportunity to meet the expectations of stakeholders on the other, but without accepting RILED constraints, which can be superficially comforting and reassuring, but at the cost of suppressing creative excellence."

"So we are agreed," said Claudia, "we can and should aim for as many design management ideals as possible, but be realistic about what is currently achieved." "That's what matters most," interrupted Mohan, "the actual worth of design work is not solely based on the balance between engineering ideals that are realised and those that are not. Worth is the balance of positive over negatives, and they don't come from just one disciplinary or professional value system. Other values in play can change the balance of worth across a mix of creative, management and engineering ideals, with each met to varying extents at varying points in a project." "You know," Soyoung added, "that even the most famous advocate of rational design, Herb Simon, had stated in his 1969 first edition of *Sciences of the Artificial* that his preferred 'science of design' should be an 'analytic, partly formalizable, partly empirical, teachable doctrine about the design process.' So, if it can only be *partly* formalizable and empirical, what is the rest? Or is his science of design only one part of design, with its non-scientific complement on an equal footing? Now, engineering and management values can be readily stated, such as intelligence, knowledge, evidence, objectivity, reliability, replication, rigour, requirements, completeness, generation, prediction, and control. Creative design values are less rarely and consistently stated, but I would expect to see exploration, experience, intuition, subjectivity, risk, originality, flexibility, framing, openness, ideation, connections, surprises, and freedom."

"My, my, you are an erudite passionate bunch!" joked Claudia, "you can't sum up without citing, but I think that we've had enough of academic research for a while. With your agreement, I'd like to call some very special witnesses, the CloudBooks team." All agreed.

### 3.1.6   ACT 6: WHAT DO THE AWARD WINNERS THINK?

Claudia congratulated the CloudBooks team on their recent award for cloud services design and thanked them for supporting the panel. The team lead, Jo, a product manager, said that they were very happy to help. Winning awards didn't mean that you had all the answers. How design work should be managed remains a major challenge, which can be exacerbated by project managers who have never done any of the jobs in a software team, but love to impose alien methodologies that guarantee they will look like management hot shots (and blame the team when they don't). Managing such managers will remain hard without confidence and consensus on how best to integrate and nurture creative practice within software development.

Johan asked the first question, "we can see that after a first release, subsequent work happens concurrently, but could have (or was) a standard software engineering design methodology have been used for CloudBooks' first release?"

The answer was *no*. The panel decided to stop second guessing the CloudBooks team. They showed them Table 3.1 for the CloudBooks work process and asked them if it was a fair picture.

The answer was *yes*. Our panel then asked specifically if development of the first version of Cloud-Books development was similar. The answer was again yes. All four work areas had immediately come into play at project inception, as in the left column of Table 3.1.

This was the first time our panel had heard of project inception. Neither the NOOF or HCD groups or Marisela had mentioned it. Even Mohan hadn't come across it in his studies of how design creates value. He wondered if he'd missed something important and asked the CloudBooks team if they had always had a project inception. Most nodded, but Jo said that they had introduced it several years ago on the advice of their Agile coach, who had a broad knowledge of different process models. He'd worked with agile since the early days of Dynamic System Development Method (DSDM) (Plonka et al., 2014) before the Scrum avalanche.

For the project inception, Jo had planned for separate foci on each design arena. Aram asked if the team was comfortable with a concurrent multidisciplinary methodology. The answer was simple. The team had been multidisciplinary for years. No one had ever attempted to stop any discipline working while it waited for another to complete something. Anyone who could even think of that never made it past a job interview. "Tell us more," asked Mohan.

"OK," said Jo, "but there's a lot to tell." She started off by noting is It hadn't always been like that. It had taken the last dozen years or so to reach where they are now. In the early days of Cloud-Books' company, only two disciplines predominated: software engineering and marketing, with the latter contributing much to the company's spectacular growth. But over the decades, engineering and business disciplines were increasingly balanced by creative ones.

To summarize what Jo said, the panel's later write-up (with citations) noted the absence of any explicit decision to simultaneously promote creative, engineering and business values. The company had added usability to its brand values, ostensibly as a vital differentiator, but actually to keep up with younger nimbler competition. However, with the web and mobile, it became impossible for any software product-service company to succeed without strong input from visual and interaction designers. As the ratio of designers to developers rose (Field, 2017), creative practices gradually took hold. This trend accelerated rapidly in the last decade (Field, 2017) and brought a job for Marisela.

The company's practice on UX expanded beyond usability and usage to aesthetics and general design quality. CloudBooks became the spearhead product with an early move to agile. The company saw CloudBooks as its future and let it dial back on some engineering and management norms from their first few decades. There were still tensions, especially given the glory with which marketing had covered itself. The CloudBooks team was given its own separate physical work area and was given headcount to recruit graduates and experienced professionals with creative design degrees.

Mohan recognised that Takeuchi and Nonaka's (1986) overlapping development phases has been established early, and then *organizational transfer of learning* and *multi-learning* moved things forward, enabling more *self-organizing project teams* and more *tolerance of instability*. He needed to ask about *subtle management control* though. "There's more of it," said Jo, "but we'd welcome even more subtle less old school bosses."

Jo explained how a range of possibilities and considerations were surfaced during a week-long inception workshop A multidisciplinary team was gathered and present most of the time. They began working in mixed discipline groups with a "purge" of whatever anyone thought could be relevant. Each group of six used the 6-3-5 Brainwriting approach (Warfield et al., 1975) to establish initial scopes for each work area. Everyone had a blank sheet of paper on which they wrote any three things that came into their head about cloud-based accounts and business support. They then passed their paper clockwise and received another sheet from their left, to which they added three more things, either in response to items already on the sheet, independently, or both. When each sheet arrived back at its initial writer, there were 18 items on it. The six sheets of paper were passed around the whole group five times. By the end, the six sheets of paper contained up to 90 items each, a potential 540 items in total for each group.

Jo explained that the aim of brainwriting is to write down what you already are aware of. It is thus a "purge" and not a brainstorming method focused solely on generating original ideas. However, there is an ideation element to it, as new ideas do occur during it. Aram had asked about Dorst's (2017) assertion that "expert designers NEVER brainstorm" (p. 26). Jo's reply was that there were relatively few expert designers on the inception team, but some of them did come up with new ideas during brainwriting. It would have been embarrassing if every new idea had come from the non-designers!

Next, each group sorted their session items into their four work areas of Development, Strategy, Evaluation and User Research. Duplicates were removed or merged. Most remaining merged and sorted items related to development and user research, with very few on evaluation. With their initial list of things to consider in place, each group began specialist work.

The UX specialists added relevant insights about beneficiaries to an *Empathy Map* (Siegel and Dray, 2019). Product management, designers, and senior developers used items of relevance to them to form a *Value Proposition Canvas* (Osterwalder et al., 2014). As input to this canvas, product management had drawn up an initial list of beneficiaries' *Jobs To Be Done* (Kalbach, 2019) and discussed it with the UX specialists. For the rest of the week, the UX specialists fleshed out best guess *personas* and a user research plan; product management developed a *roadmap* for CloudBooks; and the IxD/developer team selected product and service ideas from the value proposition canvas for future design sprints (Knapp et al., 2016).

Each group presented their progress towards the end of each day, with everyone asking questions and giving feedback. The Interaction Designers presented speculative wireframes throughout the week for discussion. On the last day, a set of *user stories* was written to prime the backlog for an agile process (Cockton, 2016a). There was also discussion on whether current evaluation practices needed revision in the light of the user research plan, roadmap, and user stories. A planned increase in user feedback channels from each Cloudworks webpage and social media was also discussed in relation to how this would be managed as additional potential evaluation data. They wanted to avoid Mintzberg's (1994) *Fallacy of Predetemination* here, knowing that upcoming business conditions could not be confidently predicted.

At the end of inception, initial work areas had been fleshed out to different extents, with some initial connections formed between them. User stories were in the form *role needs feature for reason* (Cockton, 2016a), which was a three-way connection between their work areas of user research, development, and strategy. More informal tentative connections were made during activities, presentations and discussions, e.g., via the Jobs To Be Done resource.

Design progress was evidenced by sorted and merged item lists, empathy map, personas, user research plans, jobs to be done, value proposition canvas, speculative wireframes, and a backlog of user stories. Team members also took away tacit memories of discussions, but no shared big picture. Even so, Mohan, Aram, and Johan could all see that the CloudBooks team were ahead of the game. Aram asked the CloudBooks team if they thought that their process could be improved. They answered that many design activities did not fulfil their potential, so they wanted:

- a more systematic way to plan and focus the work within their four different work areas;

- better ways to integrate across them; and

- approaches to design work that would make management comfortable with instability and exercise more subtle control, trusting the team to deliver software capabilities and user experiences beyond the imagination of anyone in marketing or management.

The CloudBooks team's expertise and experience had let them do most of the talking, in contrast to the NOOF and HCD groups. The panel didn't need to ask many questions, but focused on taking copious notes and noting links to the research literature as they wrote. They thanked the team for sharing their knowledge. They had enough to get on with writing their report.

Mohan did wonder about how they'd not seen much written about inception. Johan thought that it may be because engineering and HCD process diagrams have projects appearing from nowhere, as if project teams are handed blank slates. In HCD, design direction cannot be set until users and their tasks are fully understood (Gould and Lewis, 1985). This isn't how design projects work. Most of a project team will not even sit down in a meeting, never mind get to carry out usage context research, until senior management gives a new project a green or amber light. However, when it comes to getting a balance in a project, inception is the best place to start! A focus on inception can improve HCD work within agile methodologies (Ardito et al., 2016).

This reminded Mohan of a story from Marc Steen (2008) about a mobile computing project involving the Dutch police. Participant observation made it clear that the biggest problem was new wool uniforms. The police had no problems with their previous cotton uniforms. Mohan told the panel that since Marc and his team were so user-centred, they stopped designing innovative mobile applications and instead designed new uniforms to combine the benefits of the old cotton and the new wool uniforms. To achieve this, they would retrain for three years to become work wear designers, but nothing's too much for HCD. The panel looked shocked.

"I'm joking again," said Mohan, "of course that was too much." Marc's project team already had a R&D contract to develop mobile applications, so they could not be wholly user-centred, only selectively so. This highlights a major problem for HCD, which is that most projects start off with decisions about the form of artefact to be designed (Cockton, 2012a). Once you've chosen a technology and a specific craft practice, you cannot be 100% human-centred. A big chunk of the team's souls has already been sold to the Stuff Monster. A new project begins, as Fallman (2003) clearly identified, "in a specific design situation … that … locates the design process in a world which is already crammed with people, artifacts, and practices, each with their own histories, identities, goals, and plans." The Stuff Monster strolls in alongside an organisation's existing process, palette and playbook, along with any market intelligence practices in organisations that sell. Each take a cut of a team's souls.

"Hang on," said Mohan loudly, "I've remembered now. I've not seen inception mentioned before, but something very much like it was key to 1980s and 1990 Japanese innovation practice. Inception is what Umemoto et al. (2004) referred to as 'frontloading', where 'all project members participate [in] the earlier phases of the development process and find as many problems as possible.' However, there does need to be some sort of steer and focus. At inception, there will be assumptions about technologies, design practices, and product strategy, as well as expectations for UX practices in HCD friendly organisations. All design arenas get primed."

Soyoung added that this has been understood now for four decades ago. Darke's (1979) study of housing scheme architects showed that their initial ideas spanned more than one design arena, which helped them to focus their work. This "primary generator" had elements of Dorst's WHAT, HOW, and OUTCOME evidence, but Darke's case studies also had *negative* generators that keep options in play (i.e., stop premature dismissal). Dorst's WHAT can be a "generating thing" (the reverse of his logical frame), e.g., in Darke's case studies sites provided extensive initial direction. For both Dorst and Darke, before criteria can become part of a frame or primary generator, they must become explicit. Regardless of content in terms of design arenas, Darke's primary generators

*give rise to a proposed solution or conjecture, which makes it possible to clarify the detailed requirements as the conjecture is tested to see how far they can be met. … in most cases the design concept was arrived at before the requirements had been worked out in detail, and necessarily so, because these requirements could only become operational in the context of a particular solution.*

"Just as in Dym et al. (2014), design concepts precede requirements," Mohan continued, "the start of a project establishes an initial scope across all design arenas. We need to teach design processes that start with multiple design arenas from the very outset and keep them all in scope for as long as necessary." "I agree," said Claudia, "so let's get that and everything else down in our report."

## 3.2    SOMETHING MAGIC HAPPENS

We cannot have it all. We cannot rigorously plan creative work because its outcomes, options, and approaches cannot be fully known in advance. Such knowledge is possible for many tame problems, which involve minimal creative framing, but even here problems such as the proof of Fermat's Last Theory, which was easily stated in a margin but took centuries to solve, clearly defy the rational planning of Gantt charts, milestones and resource allocation. Although there is no hard line between tame and wicked problems, the latter do require us to relax on engineering ideals until a wicked problem begins to settle down into a tame one.

The panel were uncomfortable with seeing disciplinary value systems as mutually exclusive or paradoxical. Each gives a different axiological account of design, and each differs in its expectations of empirical validity. Clearly, what creative designers actually do is an empirical question, but what they should do, given their obligations to stakeholders (imposed but not always accepted), is an axiological one that concerns values of one form or another (i.e., moral, ethical, legal—and from the perspectives of designers, clients, beneficiaries, and maleficaries).

Soyoung looked at her notes. "It's clear that design isn't a shape and it hasn't got a centre. It's also clear that we need to balance all disciplinary practices in design. We need to respect as many engineering and management values as possible, while remaining compatible with the realities of creative design practice." "Can we do that though?" asked Aram, who pointed out that HCD and engineers' values differ from those of creative designers, who focus on outcomes rather than process, with design excellence judged by results, not procedures. "Why, in the absence of actual evidence for any extensive viability of rational or scientific design practices, does each decade bring new advocates who are going to sort out design, scientifically, managerially or both?"

Aram replied that engineering designers themselves haven't helped. Petroski (1994) noted their notoriety for avoiding discussion of their methodology. Free use is made of the term "engineering method" for which "precise definitions remain curiously elusive and is yet to be articulated in a universally agreed upon form." His research into structural design failures draws on searching public inquiries that require realism and detachment, where there is no place for zealous promotion of any idealised design methodology. He also notes how inquiries have not called for better science supported by better computational tools, but for non-numerical "improved design-thinking skills" including improved self-criticism, but "the first and most indispensable design tool is judgement."

"The answer may be millennia old," said Johan. Gedenryd (1998) carried out an extensive review of the sequential models of rational behaviour from ancient Greek philosophy to post 1950 mathematics and cognitive science. Given millennia of accepting such models, it can thus seem obvious that we must first fully define a problem before attempting any solution. The logical order here is beyond doubt. The Western world has predominantly thought this way for millennia. Creative designers have somehow managed to think differently despite this, but so have the mathematicians whose proofs are the mistaken model for sequential analysis-synthesis models. Analysis and synthesis for contemporary non-routine mathematical proofs and calculations are concurrent (Gedenryd, 1998), and may have been even for Pappus of Alexandria, despite his implication in serialising rational thought. The serialisation is much clearer for *praxis* in Aristotle, for whom rational *action* (Cockton, 2018) needs a clear goal and a *plan of action* to definitely achieve that goal. This restricts deliberation on a plan to "things that are in our power," but in creative work what is in our power may only be discovered through experiment rather than a plan that is known to work in advance. While rational action may be an extension of rational thinking (Gedenryd, 1998), creative practice cannot be.

Johan jumped from ancient Greece to the mid-20th century. Gedenryd notes how the mathematician Polya added a plan within the "natural" order of "analysis first and synthesis afterwards," i.e., in between analysis and synthesis, and holding them together. As design methodology developed in the decades after Polya's (1945) book, requirements replaced this plan as the starting point for rational synthesis.

"That's very interesting," said Aram, "to be practically viable, analysis must interface with synthesis, which must interface with evaluation. Yet, there is very limited evidence of clear interfaces between the stages of sequential engineering design that let the outputs from one phase be systematically 'translated' into the outputs of the next. Nor is there evidence of outputs for a following phase being completely 'generated' from a previous one. Such practices would be objective and systematic, without dependence on creative flair, which at least partially explains their attractiveness within engineering and managerial value systems. Unfortunately, tame problems aside, there is no basis in fact for the actual existence of the wishful one-way arrows between sequential phases. Nevertheless, engineering and management processes fetishize boxes and arrows. Their attraction to those who must be seen to manage is clear. They are parts of managerial practices that can prioritise financial engineering over productive work (Weber, 2017).

"Don't underestimate the power of rational models," said Soyoung, "the underlying values have been with us for millennia and achieved dominance with the rationalists of the Scientific Revolution in the 17th century, when methods were sought that would guarantee truth and identify falsehood. Descartes was convinced that Pappus of Alexandria and other ancient geometers had had a method for analysis that he had kept secret, forcing Descartes to rediscover one. Even today, Lash and Wynne (1994) have noted how the culture of Scientism creates false claims and expectations in society at large about research *methods* that are vital and superior. While the constant stream of technological and other science-based advances is clear historical evidence for the power of scientific *values*, beliefs about "scientific method" are poorly evidenced in the past and present, as well suffering from clear philosophical limitations. Similarly, we can find encouraging evidence in the past and present of engineering design projects that have delivered on time, to specification and within budget (and not always simply because their problems were tame). However, as with claimed simple versions of "the" scientific method, there is also much evidence of such methodologies failing with severe consequences (Petroski, 1994). As Gedenryd (1998) pointed out, design methodology was so confident in analysis-synthesis-evaluation approaches "that there was hardly a need to ask if they worked, much less to test whether they did." This was especially so because it is not easy at all to think of an alternative to linear rationality, however much gaps in positions on it are exposed."

"You're right," said Claudia, "and this power is often exercised through language. Rittel and Webber's (1973) use of the word 'wicked' collaborates with scientific and managerial values by labelling untameable problems as evil. This puzzles me because Rittel and Webber had such a well-informed argument for the pervasiveness of wicked problems in creative design work. What I see here is the power of scientific and managerial value systems within design theory. In the face of evidence that many design 'problems' are not fully defined until a 'solution' has been accepted, Cockton (2017) notes that the language of problems, solutions and deviant wickedness remains entrenched."

Soyoung continued that it had not helped to implicitly see creative work as wickedly deviant. Few denied the actual truth of the reality here, but its desirability remained in doubt because wickedness affronts scientific and managerial values. "I've got an idea though," continued Soyoung, recalling Dym's (1994) definition of Engineering Design above, where "form and function achieve stated objectives and satisfy specified constraints." "You know," she said, "wicked problems can satisfy Dym's definition by stating final objectives and specifying acknowledged constraints *after* a solution has been finalised. Whole diagrams of engineering design processes indicate clearly that objectives (requirements) and constraints are specified as soon as possible, but Dym's 1994 definition leaves timings unspecified. Design work could thus be like mathematical proof work, with the aim to reach a connected well-bridged imago (Davies and Talbot, 1987) by whatever means. As long as a final artefact meets a highly desirable purpose, the means to such ends are secondary."

"I think you are really onto something there," said Mohan, "it's like a mathematical proof, which is judged by the logic of its steps as written. As Gedenryd (1998) argued, 'regardless of how it was discovered,' a longstanding position within Software Engineering (Parnas and Clements, 1986). Surely what is good enough for Gauss' queen of sciences is good enough for design work? We need to avoid naïve positions on what is logical or contradictory. Wild (not 'wicked') problems can be seen as involving paradoxes, especially between stakeholders' value positions. Creative design thrives on dissolving paradoxes (Davies and Talbot, 1987; Dorst, 2015, 2017), which usually turn out to be more apparent than real. Apparently conflicting values between stakeholders can be transcended by a design that keeps everyone happy (e.g., care circles and clinicians; Doherty et al., 2000). Problems arise from unmanaged bias rather than irresolvable paradoxes."

"I really like that," said Aram, "designing for wild (not 'wicked') problems is Creative, Reflective, Exploratory, and Aesthetic in its Moves (CREAM; Cockton, 2017), but none of this rules out reaching outcomes that can be critically and rigorously defended. We can legitimately be RILED once the CREAM has run out. But we must live with instability, complexity, and uncertainty, just like mathematicans do when working on proofs. A proof is hyperrational once completed, an archetype of reason, but coming up with a polished proof is a creative progression—not a process—that no sensible person would prescribe in advance. If mathematicians can have such freedom, then so can designers."

"I love that," said Claudia, "progression—not a process. This has been a wonderful sharing of insights and knowledge. It's felt like a good design session. To an outsider watching on, it must look like we've been rambling here and there without any purpose or plan, but look where we've got to through all this discussion and sharing. We can think of design work as being like forming a mathematical proof that falls into place in what looks like a random order, but at the end, everything flows from start to end. Of course, design moves won't be like the steps in a mathematical proofs. We're not replacing equals with equals, but moves are still valid. I like the analogy. Something magic has happened."

Claudia continued, "We need to start on our recommendations. This isn't going to be easy given what one of the NOOF group said: there's no doubt about what good design is, but designers get it wrong by being lazy and ignorant and not following methods and process correctly. There's no need for human science or theory of any form, especially from trouble making sophists who would argue forever. Science already has all the answers, as long as one is not lazy and can be managed to work hard to the highest standards." "Absolutely," said Mohan, "and 50 years of research into design can all be completely ignored. I suppose there's no arguing with any of that." "It's frustrating," added Soyoung, "we know this 50 years of research into design very well and it's consistent." "We're not lazy either," said Daniela, "if anything it's people who can't be critical about language and evidence, and who won't reflect on the concepts that they are using and the values underpinning them who are lazy. They've just got their heads in the sand. They want an easy managerial or professional life and won't engage with difficult issues." "Office politics and project crises apart," added Mohan, "and that can take up a lot of their energy." "I hear you," said Claudia, "now let's wrap up."

## 3.3    A BALANCED DESIGN MANIFESTO

"I propose the following issues for a new software design curriculum," began Claudia. "People can add engineering in there somewhere as long as it displaces nothing below. Now let's put our veil of ignorance on and consider the following:

1. What would you see as the main areas of design work?

2. If you had to choose an order for design work, what, if anything, would the progression be? Would work be concurrent or sequential?

3. How would work be integrated? Does concurrent or sequential working make a difference?

4. Would you want to fix interfaces in advance to ease integration of design work?

5. Would you want a model of design work to knowingly and deliberately miss things out?

6. Would you be happy with aimless wandering with no sense of progress?

7. If you were presented with a vocabulary of problems, solutions, phases and transformations, would you feel that you could work effectively with it.

I'd like each of us to be responsible for discussing a question each with everyone and then present the consensus answer."

The panel worked the next day, rotating through the questions. There was still a lot of discussion. It was a good job the NOOF group didn't have to listen. Claudia presented her answer first.

1. If we'd never seen Heskett's (2005) account of choices and design outcomes, we'd probably come up with something similar. There are clearly means and ends, as in all human activities; those means will be used by someone to achieve ends that matter to them; and we can assess how much those ends are achievable with the given means.

Aram answered next:

2. We saw no basis for any fixed order for work on different design areas. Creative work must be concurrent, even without knowledge of primary generators and frontloading. You can't know in advance when and how ideas will emerge and how they will develop. Fixed sequences have no obvious positive creative benefit. Any benefits are managerial and largely imagined. These are offset by risks of losing ideas that make designs much more worthwhile.

Soyoung continued:

3. We have no idea how work will be integrated, but behind our veil of ignorance we expect integration to happen. We can't see any reason why it wouldn't

Johan followed.

4. Our answer is the same as Aram's. We can't see how fixed interfaces and creative work could ever be compatible, and given Soyoung's answer, this doesn't seem to matter. If integration happens, then interfaces will be formed as part of the connections that are made between different areas of design work.

Daniela presented her answer.

5. You can't have a veil of total ignorance. People know about gender, race, abilities, tastes, wealth, position in society, and the like behind Rawls veil of ignorance. We would know enough to see that there is no good reason for missing things out of a model just to keep things simple. After all, omissions may deliberately mask.

Mohan was next.

6. Of course not. There's no basis for assuming that a lack of fixed sequence, interfaces and integrating connections would result in aimless wandering. We can balance work across different areas and much design work will lead to some progress, which can and should be tracked to gain and retain the trust of clients and managers.

"Oh," said Claudia, "we have seven questions, but there are only six of us. I think we've answered the seventh question. If we don't start with a lexicon including problem, solution, phase, transformation, and other controlling words, I can't see why we'd add them. Design work areas generalises the first three and connections is far less presumptuous than the last. I propose the following manifesto for all forms of engineering and media innovation:

1. work areas for balanced design address: means, ends, beneficiaries, and evaluation;

2. concurrent working is the norm across areas of design work, sequence is the exception;

3. connections between work areas are created, not preformed;

4. interfaces between work areas can be prepared to support connection work;

5. design progression models should be complete at every level of their abstractions;

6. design work should be tracked across work areas in ways to reveal progress; and

7. misleading RILED language needs to be retired.

The first manifesto position replicates Chapter 2's answer to the first question in Chapter 1 on design work areas, which was based on the design research literature, with an *a priori* one

(Cockton, 2010a), but no alternatives to the areas in Table 1.1 have yet been offered. The second and fifth positions above answer the third question in Chapter 1 on standard process structures: there are no standard regimented phase sequences. The only correct structure is a concurrent complete *progression* (within which sequence is a special case, which is the only time that iteration is a meaningful concept). The third and fourth positions above answer the second question in Chapter 1 on how design work areas relate to each other: connections are created between prepared interfaces. All these answers are very high level, and as with all creative work, the major function of an answer is to spawn further questions.

4. What forms and levels of abstraction would a comprehensive model of design work have?

5. What sort of connections and interfaces would be in this model?

6. What forms of tracking would a new model support?

7. What does progress look like when design work is tracked with support from a new model?

The panel discussion has provided additional question to those asked in Chapter 1 and partially answered in Chapter 2. Question 5 above simplifies (and replaces) Question 2 in Chapter 1: relations and transitions are subsumed under connections. Chapter 4 addresses all questions except the sixth above, which Chapter 5 addresses along with the last question. Chapter 4 builds on initial answers in Chapter 2 and insights from the design practice research above.

"Now," said Mohan, we'll look stupid if our manifesto turns out to be just as unworkable as standard and textbook RILED processes. I'll be relieved once someone writes a book on it." "Someone will have to," said Claudia, "if not, we could all stay stuck in a nonsense world of boxes, arrows, amateur project managers, cut down versions for teaching, and similar distortions that cannot erase the realities that they seek to hide."

The remainder of this Book 1 and chapters in Book 2 (Cockton, 2020b) propose a series of responses to the above manifesto. The next chapter addresses complete models with concurrent design arenas (1, 2, and 5) and begins development of a new vocabulary to discard RILED influences (7). Chapter 5 addresses tracking (6) via high-level representations of design work, supported by initial considerations of connections (3) and interfaces (4), and adds to the new vocabulary (7). Chapters 2 and 3 (Cockton, 2020b) address supporting approaches and resources for work within design arenas, including interfaces (4). Chapter 4 (Cockton, 2020b) addresses integration (3) through connections (5). Case studies in Chapter 5 (Cockton, 2020b) and Chapter 6's (Cockton, 2020b) conclusions offer a basis for management trust.

CHAPTER 4

# Status not Process: Abstract Design Situations as Snapshots of Design Work

Chapter 3's *Balanced Design Manifesto* espouses seven theses. The fifth is that models of design progression should be complete at every level of abstraction. Closures like "every" cannot be fully addressed without adopting positions on the highest and lowest levels of abstraction, but we begin with a first abstraction in this chapter. Before this, the nature of work areas (first manifesto position) as design arenas is first developed in the next two sections, drawing on political theory. A new structure, the Abstract Design Situation (ADS) is then proposed. The high abstraction level allows modelling of three major design paradigms, with their sequences and concurrency when progressing designs (second manifesto position). Next, a higher level of abstraction lets a new family of concurrent post-centric design paradigms be realised from one template structure.

The template structure is complex and harder to grasp than Dorst's (2015) frames, which can capture a design strategy in a single metaphor. However, before this pragmatic form of frame, Dorst first proposes a logical form that contains latent sequence that would be best removed. This is achieved by a new *axiofact* concept that focuses design on connections and progressions.

This chapter's analyses accumulate responses to the last manifesto position, identifying misleading RILED language and replacing it with younger words. The need to replace RILED language follows from continued use of linear process models that have been knowingly incomplete for over five decades, omitting backtracking, concurrency, and other breaks from iterated sequences because these make processes harder to express, teach, and manage:

> *Given that there are feedback loops and that we will reiterate some tasks, why didn't we include them in [the] Figure …? As important as feedback and iteration are, it is also important not to be overly distracted by these adaptive characteristics when learning about and doing design for the first time* (Dym et al., 2014).

> *The stages are overlapping and often confused, with frequent returns to early stages when difficulties are encountered and obscurities found* (Archer, 1963/4).

The approach taken in this chapter is to increase the level of abstraction, even though highly abstract theories have a poor record in design research (Gaver, 2011; Löwgren, 2013). Dorst (2017) contrasts the authenticity of concrete design situations with overly abstract design process models. Within HCI, Carroll (2000) has valued how scenarios have designers "interacting intimately with the concrete elements of the situation." Similarly, Fallman's (2003) pragmatic account of design focuses on *specific* design situations, in contrast to his conservative account's process models. Abstraction can disappoint when compared to situated details from empirical studies. For Lawson (1980), the evidence was that all design projects are unique, which warns against naive abstraction. However, the problem has not been one of abstraction. It is one of lacunation.

Realistic progression models must be *comprehensive*, and shown to be so through something like Popper's (1959/1934) *falsification*. While no scientific theory can conclusively be proved true, it can survive attempts at falsification. Similarly, progression models should survive *lacunation* attempts to find gaps in them (in biology, *lacunation* is the formation of cavities). Gaps have been deliberately left in RILED process models.

If we start from well-documented creative practice rather than management values, then we should be able to avoid gaps. Dorst's (2017) *concrete design situation* is a starting point for a better abstraction, that of a *situation*. Can we abstract over concrete design situations, instead of over work order? What would an *abstract design situation* comprise?

## 4.1   ABSTRACTION, STATUS, AND SITUATIONS

Concrete design work is continuously constituted as a set of active design arenas and achieved connections between them. If we only consider *whether* (not *how*) a design arena is active and *what* (not *how*) connections have been made, we have a basis for a very high-level abstraction, capturing the current status of design work as an abstract snapshot.

An ADS combines a *set* of design arenas with cumulative *connections* between them. The two key words in this definition are *set* and *connections*. We will examine design arenas before considering connections between them.

Design arenas can thus replace problems and solutions as fundamental constructs for design work without imposing order on how design work *progresses*. This avoids the ambiguities in Chapter 3 on whether ISO9241-210 requirements are in the problem or solution space. Design arenas rename Heskett's (2005) *types of choices that result in outcomes* as:

- *purpose*: choices of "ends;"

- *artefacts*: choices of "initial decision or concepts," "how these are implemented," "how ends can be achieved" [means];

- *beneficiaries*: choices of "for whose advantage;" and

- *evaluations*: choices of "by what means we evaluate ... benefit."

Like problems and solutions, design arenas co-evolve, but with no ambiguities on what is in the problem or solution space. The word "arena" is an important part of a new lexicon for design work. Its initial use was pragmatic: "types of choices that result in outcomes" is too cumbersome.

As a metaphor, arena refers to an enclosed space, originally a competitive one for sport, combat, attention, argument, or discussion.

## 4.1.1   ARENAS AS SYMBOLIC SPACES

Before we add "arena" to a new lexicon for design work, its uses need to be reviewed. It has very general use in design. For example, Junginger (2017) notes "a growing recognition that the main arena in which design is practiced is not business, but the organization." Her broadening of the arena for design work is not physical, but organisational, covering public and voluntary as well as private sectors.

Arena metaphors have developed in political science, especially for policy and risk, including areas such as planning, the policy arena with public risks where the Wicked Problem concept originated (Rittel and Weber, 1973). The social arena concept was established in the 1960s by Theodore Lowi. He argued that there is no unique political process (just as there is no unique design process), and so replaced process (temporal) with arena (territorial). For Kitschelt (1980), a *social* arena is a *symbolic* rather than physical *location* of political actions. It subsumes organisations (unlike Junginger's usage above). Another use of arena (Bourdieu, 1984) is synonymous with a non-homogeneous social-spatial "field," where people manoeuvre and struggle in pursuit of desirable resources. Renn (1992) added theatre metaphors such as stage, audience and critic.

Design arenas are not only symbolic but also *material* locations. They are *sociomaterial* locations of design actions (ATELIER, 2011). This materiality includes workspaces, and is thus also socio-spatial, like Bourdieu's arenas. The target artefacts and *co-products* of design work (Carroll, 2000), e.g. personas, design rationales, and scenarios, also have material forms.

Renn identifies a wide range of arenas, drawing on authorities such Parsons and Peters. Some are very high level: domestic and foreign; economics, politics, society, culture, and science (Parsons); administration, judiciary, science, and mass media (Peters). Others are more specific: sales, policy, and healthcare. Some arenas nest in hierarchies: home help within healthcare; maritime insurance within insurance; commercial mortgage within mortgages; and insurance and mortgages within finance. Similarly, design arenas have overlapping hierarchies of subarenas. Bourdieu's fields are also hierarchical and nest.

For Renn (1992), a social arena is a realm where important events unfold. We reinterpret it for design arenas.

- Several arenas may exist within a policy *field*. Similarly, several arenas can exist within a design *programme*, which is the R&D progression across all versions of a product. Dorst's (2015) "field" in his frame creation model is close to an anyficiaries arena with links to purpose. We rename Renn's broader concept of "field" to "programme" to avoid confusion with Dorst's usage from Bourdieu.

- There are multiple actors with responsibilities (but no scripts) within an arena, and multiple stages from which they communicate with audiences. Similarly, many actors can work within a design arena, and across its subarenas, communicating through a range of co-products with a range of stakeholders.

- Arenas interact while preserving their autonomy, but outcomes are indeterminate, especially when they result from innovative behaviours. Similarly, design arenas are separable enough within a design programme, but interact unpredictably due to adventitious design phenomena.

- Arenas are subject to formal and informal modifiable rules. Bourdieu's fields have rules.

- Resources are mobilised intentionally: in risk arenas to influence policy; and in design arenas to influence design direction. Resources are pursued in Bourdieu's arena, with social, economic, and cultural capital deployed to gain them. In design, resources are mobilised, but their potential functions need to be activated to be realised. Activation is often adventitious, i.e., resulting from external factors or chance.

Although we consider design arenas to be a very high-level concept, Renn's more specific uses have him regard social arenas as "meso level," matching Löwgren's (2013) preference for intermediate level knowledge as the level of theory in HCI. However, design arenas are at a single level of abstraction, whereas Löwgren's examples range from fairly high-level concepts and themes, via design methods and tools, to patterns, design guidelines, and usability heuristics. Löwgren acknowledges that even a single example here, design methods, and tools, almost spans the whole abstraction range from particular artefacts towards general HCI theory. Such a range does not aid critical reflection, so for our new lexicon we aim for more homogeneous families of abstractions.

It thus is reasonable to consider design programmes as a creative field with arenas nesting within them, and subarenas within them in turn. After all, design is a form of social arena. It shares many of the features of the social arenas of risk. However, worthwhile products balance positives and negatives, combining opportunity proliferation and protection with Renn's risk reduction and management. Opportunities and risks are balanced against each other.

Arenas thus have formal and informal rules, responsibilities, actors, stages, audiences, and resources, which may be allocated, created, or contested. Repurposing a politics concept is apt given how political design can be, e.g., as in giving "real control of the user interface to the people who had responsibility for usability" (Gould and Lewis, 1985). Also, policy and design have been converging for at least the last decade, with policies being designed along with the services that will implement them (Junginger, 2017). As a result, we are beginning to see more synergies between design and politics.

Design work thus operates within a programme, via integrated arenas, with subarenas, actors, stages, audiences, rules, responsibilities, and resources. Renn's "fundamental axiom is that resource availability determines the degree of influence." Design resources propel design arenas, which we next consider.

## 4.2    DESIGN ARENAS

Design arenas are a name for Heskett's (2005) forms of design choice (Section 2.3). The naming turned out to be adventitious, since a survey of the use of "arena" in design and elsewhere found a rendezvous with political science. This has provided a family of concepts and metaphors for understanding design arenas as *sociomaterial* locations of design work. Renn's (1992) elaboration of his social arena concept produces a theory with a clear focus on structure, emphasising resources and their impacts. This has general applicability to design: resources are the means through which actors have influence.

Renn identifies five resources of major relevance: money, power, social influence, value commitment, and evidence. While his examples all relate to the politics of risk, such as the environment and nuclear power, these resources are not only political, but also economic, social, cultural, and scientific. All matter for design programmes, which are both enabled and limited to some extent by: budgets (economics); management and client power (organisational politics); trust and prestige (social influence); solidarity and cultural unity (disciplinary value commitments); and scientific methodologies and rhetoric (evidence gathering and its implications).

Renn's account of evidence as a resource is relevant to both risk arenas and multi-disciplinary design, since evidence is relative and pluralistic in both, but can be tested against reality. "Evidence is not identical with truth." For Renn, "truth" is a universal ideal, while "evidence" is a claim to truth based on methodological rules and accepted theoretical knowledge. Evidence is often ambiguous, from multiple incommensurable sources, with availability making its value subject to inflation and deflation. Design work too has to cope with incommensurability and inflation/deflation, as well as ambiguity and incompleteness (Kolko, 2010).

Evidence must be agreed on, but its accuracy for possible outcomes may remain unknown until decisions have been taken and acted on. However, design time scales are typically much shorter than, for example, environmental risks. Evaluation evidence can be timely, even when not clear cut.

Successful influence requires more than one resource. Money and power within hierarchies are not enough. Persuasion and cultural meaning are needed. "All actors need a minimal reservoir of each resource" (Renn, 1992). Power must be shared in exchange for evidence or value commitment. Such exchanges are not part of a zero-sum game, because new resources can be created or accessed. However, exchange does bring risks of losing resources without gaining others.

Successful resource mobilization depends on perception of overall performance in several arenas. "Hot" issues can be used to piggyback other claims. In design, accessibility, user experience, and sustainability are all hot issues that actors use to gain leverage. Also, local issues can become symbols for broader ones. In design, a user-centred issue can be part of a much broader respect and concern for people that has UX specialists "fighting for the user."

Successful resource mobilization also depends on communication, especially to generate trust and commitment. Resources are used for different purposes, and thus have different potential functions to be realised in practice. Several resource functions have already been indicated above. Corresponding functions identified for design work (Cockton, 2013a) are juxtaposed in (brackets): communication (expressive), persuasion (performative), trust (affiliative), value commitment (ameliorative), and evidence (informative). To mobilize a resource is to activate and then realize its potential functions.

We now apply these concepts to the four design arenas identified in Section 2.3, using a framework adapted from social arena research, i.e., subarenas, rules, audiences, actors, stages, responsibilities, and resources.

### 4.2.1    AN ARENA FOR EVALUATION WORK

The *evaluation* arena has *stages* and *audiences* for presentations. Audiences for reports may be the core design team, or a wider group that can include clients, sponsors, a steering board or even the general public: the *Common Industry Format* (ISO, 2019b) supports public comparison of usability of competitor products.

Analytical and empirical evaluation practices differ in social prestige, economic costs (time and money), and disciplinary value commitments. Evaluation subarenas can be methodological, e.g.: testing, surveys, instrumentation, log analysis, inspection, or modelling. Engineering evaluation can be empirical, but is primarily analytical, calculating optimal design parameters via science-based methods. HCD evaluation is human science-based: user testing resources have roots in experimental psychology, and field-testing resources have theirs in work ethnography. Resources are often combined into *approaches* (e.g., user testing, field testing). Approaches can involve *rules* such as research ethics. Practical evaluation resources can be devalued by inappropriate value commitments, for example, dubious attempts to compare HCD evaluation methods in psychological experiments (Gray and Salzman, 1998). Scientific resources can thus be misapplied.

We prefer the term "approach" to "method," since the latter is typically not in place as a complete public procedure that can be used "as is" without adaptation or augmentation. Inspection approaches were developed in both computer and cognitive science. "Big Data" has brought statistical analyses of usage data, making analysis of millions of user sessions on large platforms affordable at a scale that would be impossible for user testing. However, there are no methods here, only resources that can be combined once adapted and completed. Methods are strictly approaches until they are completed in use (Woolrych et al., 2011).

The human sciences (including big data) do not monopolise evaluation. Creative practices such as reflection and critique preceded them and continue to extend current practices. Much evaluation practice is creative (Cockton, 2014), e.g., the emergence of *Creative Sprints* (Garnik et al., 2014), which exploited resources such as knowledge of audience for final presentations and reports, crowd sourced usability problems, domain expertise, and a favourable physical work environment.

Designers' judgement cannot and should not be sidelined in evaluation work, despite objections from some quarters (e.g., Gould and Lewis, 1985). The span of actors involved in evaluation is thus wide, and includes UX specialists, designers, participants, analysts, and management. As with the other design arenas below, evaluation work spans several disciplines. No design arena "belongs" to a single discipline, but there are clear disciplinary and professional differences for each, and thus differences in value commitments, prestige and power. However, regardless of subarenas, rules, and disciplinary and professional resources, all actors within an evaluation arena are responsible for assessing designed artefacts' quality and performance.

## 4.2.2    AN ARENA FOR STRATEGIC DESIGN PURPOSE

*Purpose* is primarily axiological (i.e., about value not fact). A Wo-Fo provides design purpose with useful initial high-level subarenas (i.e., benefits, costs, and risks). This can draw on disciplinary practices from business (especially marketing and product/service innovation) or public administration (policy). Creative design can also foreground purpose. Norman Potter (1989), a previous generation's well-respected design educator, asked "What is good design?" and answered that "the 'goodness' or 'rightness' of a design cannot be easily estimated outside of a knowledge of its purpose." However, designer-makers may lack explicit intentions and be guided by the sculptor Henry Moore's (1934) "truth to material."

HCD can put purpose beyond deliberation when it is expected to be identified by primary user research as needs, wants, goals, tasks, etc. IxD goals may be expressed as requirements, specifications, product visions, or design briefs, according to stakeholder preferences. These differ in the extent to which design purpose is explicit as: (a) benefits to be enhanced or added and (b) costs to be reduced or risks to be averted.

In engineering, specifications may strictly describe precisely what will be realised, rather than (prescriptively) why it is desirable, reducing purpose to developing artefacts: at this extreme, the means become the end. In software engineering, requirements can be reduced to artefact specifications, rather than statements of purpose separate from any artefact used to achieve it.

Design purposes thus span from the tacit dynamic goals of designer-makers to the explicit fixed requirements of engineering design. It is thus a stretch to span all practices that set direction for purpose, especially as not all design practices stress its importance. *Motivating purposes* is one possible umbrella term to cover this arena, but it is not in common use.

Most explicit specialist approaches and resources for design purpose originate in business and innovation, e.g., unique selling propositions, value proposition canvases (Osterwalder et al., 2014), and Jobs To Be Done (Kalbach, 2019). These approaches can mix primary and secondary research in support of *design strategy* at product level, and *Strategic Design* at organisational level (Stevens and Moultrie, 2011). Strategic Design develops all design arenas and connections across all an organisation's products. Design Strategy focuses on one product. However, both practices are strategic, aiming to greatly increase the odds of success (Bradley et al., 2018). Generosity of purpose (Chapter 2) increases such odds because purpose is not a given from the outset, despite a strong tradition in Western thought that "ends" are givens, e.g., Aristotle's assertion (Gedenryd, 1998) that:

> *We deliberate not about ends but about means. For a doctor does not deliberate  whether he shall heal, nor an orator whether he shall persuade,  nor a statesman whether he shall pro-duce law and order … They  assume the end and consider how and by what means it is to be attained.*

One wonders what Aristotle would think about a design agency that always assumed "that the brief is wrong" and probed clients on what "they're actually wanting" (Stevens and Moultrie, 2011).

Framing purpose as a separate design arena with its own resources, actors, and audiences exposes the multiple contexts where it forms and evolves. Design purpose needs to consider all stakeholders. A user focus is not enough. This can bring considerations such as brand and strategy, where what begins as cross product qualities such as usability for mobile phones can significantly strengthen brand consistency and recognition (Stevens and Moultrie, 2011). Such considerations are not only commercial, there is "a growing recognition that the main arena in which design is practiced is not business, but the organization" (Junginger, 2017). The public sector has led in the adoption of, Dorst's (2015) Frame Creation mode, with the commercial sector following in markets such as healthcare, pharmaceuticals, food, and transport.

Without a separate arena for design purpose, the only basis for generosity in any paradigm is the designer's tacit intent in applied arts. In engineering, purpose gets too closely aligned with the artefact. In HCD, purpose gets too closely aligned with beneficiaries. Design purpose is not only about creating artefacts (engineering), nor is it only about meeting users' needs (HCD) or designer's visions (applied arts). Nor is it about excluding any of them. It concerns all stakeholders' interests, designers and evaluators included. It is a broad arena that benefits from the wide range of engaged actors involved in Strategic Design initiatives (Stevens and Moultrie, 2011). Whatever the sources of design purpose, resources are needed to direct work on design purpose. For example, Dorst (2015) notes that if the purpose of a night out with friends is to have a good time, imagination is needed to work out what "good time" means. Initial expressions of purpose are a resource for directing subsequent design activities that seek external evidence to validate them.

Individual actors are not enough. Renn's (1992) social arena framework needs to extend to alliances, which greatly improve the prospects for improving design quality (Convertino and Frishberg, 2020). Such alliances can communicate internally how design strategy at programme level can create value for both a business and its customers, something inherently complex that needs multidisciplinary approaches to design purpose. Internal communication must focus on both product innovation and organizational culture. Alliances greatly augment specialist design roles. At Autodesk, 1,900 employees in a company with 400 designers had set up accounts to participate in a "radical design collaboration" within 7 months of its launch (Convertino and Frishberg, 2020). This alliance of designers, marketing, engineering, and executives created stages and audiences across design arenas.

### 4.2.3 AN ARENA FOR A_TEFACTS: ARTEFACTS AND ANTEFACTS

We follow Carroll's (1990) distinction between design products and co-products. Wolf et al. (2006) similarly write of "communication artifacts that serve the end result but are not the end result themselves." In contrast, in much writing on agile development, "artefact" refers to both products and co-products. However, it is important to distinguish the main persistent output of design work from more ephemeral ones. In our new lexicon, we reserve 'artefact' for the terminal products delivered within design programmes. No judgement is made on relative worth here though. Artefacts and co-products have equal potential value and it is important to stress this, but Löwgren and Stolterman (2004) go too far when they stress knowledge co-products as "the main 'products' … intended for other members of the knowledge construction culture." If the aim is to field an artefact, then it is clearly of primary importance. If the aim it to carry out research through design, then the co-products are indeed of primary importance, including publications and exhibitions that rarely result from practical design work. However, it is also rarely the case that only the artefact is of value, as co-products often guide individual and organisational learning for future projects and programmes, and can be re-usable with or without adaptation.

Many example design artefacts above are not terminal products (e.g., sketches, specifications, models, prototypes, scenarios). In much design work, terminal products must be manufactured, fabricated, constructed, coded, or printed. In research through design, research publications may be the terminal product, rather than the antefact. We thus need another new word for our design lexicon and consider the Latin roots of *arte-fact* (Cockton, 2017): a thing *made* (factus) by some *art* (arte), as the final version of a released product or research object. However, prior partial versions, often in different material forms to the final artefact, can be called *antefacts*, a word anticipated in "features composing an (or to be) artifact" (Otero and José, 2009).

To cover both artefact and antefact, we need a comprehensive neologism, and leverage typography with a_tefacts (pronounced *ahtefacts* much as we pronounce Ms. relative to Miss and Mrs.) For the remainder of this book, we use a_tefact when both antefacts and artefacts are in scope, and antefacts or artefacts when one sense is apt.

Design approaches and resources for a_tefacts are craft dependent, i.e., fashion, graphics, products, and interactions create different material forms and thus have mostly different forms of antefact. Guidance and precedent (outstanding design exemplars) are common resources for a_tefacts.

Fallman (2003) places antefacts such as sketches and prototypes at the heart of co-evolution. Sketches and prototypes act as "stages" for sharing ideas and proposals with audiences. Prototypes can be lo-fi (e.g., paper, cardboard) or hi-fi (e.g., highly finished interactive wireframes). They may also be experiential, e.g., video envisionment. Through five decades of research into design, we understand the many valuable functions of sketching. Jones (1970) grounded the need for design methodologies in the belief that design-by-drawing was too simple for the growing complexity of the man-made world. For Gedenryd (1998), Jones saw this as a widely held belief that did not require further justification. Research on sketching has shown that it is not inherently simple and there is no apparent limit to the complexities that it can embrace (Goldschmidt, 2014).

In IxD, the a_tefact arena can draw on disciplinary practices from both creative design and software engineering. Their resources vary considerably. They span Garrett's (2002) *Elements of User Experience*. For system-driven interaction, dialogue models (Garrett's *Structure*, or workflows) originated in computer science and linguistics (Cockton, 1990, 1993). For user-driven interaction, event-oriented object models from software engineering (Cockton et al., 1996) provide one form of conceptual model (Garrett's *Scope*). Wireframes (Garrett's *Skeleton*) have their origins in the roughs, comps, or scamps of (graphic) editorial design. Garrett's *Surface* of graphics and other media is wholly the domain of creative practice, supported as and where effective by both scientific knowledge and critical humanities perspectives. Garrett's *Strategy* apart (which is purpose), we can regard his other four elements as potential architectural subarenas for a_tefacts. Other possible subarenas are enabling technologies, conventions, best practices, and current trends/fashions.

### 4.2.4    AN ARENA FOR ANYFICIARIES: BENEFICIARIES AND MALEFICIARIES

For our last design arena, we again consider the Latin root of *bene-ficiaries*: those for whom *good is done*. However, design work may not wholly focus on doing good for everyone: there may be *maleficiaries*, those to whom *harm is done*. For example, design against crime should harm criminals. As with a_tefact, we need a word to span both beneficiaries and maleficiaries. A comprehensive neologism for those for/to whom *anything is done* can be formed: *anyficiaries*. This portmanteau word covers those who are deliberately designed for or against, but also includes those who are inadvertently harmed, e.g., through exclusion of the old, young, disabled, or someone diverse in other ways from a design norm (e.g., face tracking recognition software that only works with Caucasians). As with a_tefacts, for the rest of this book, we will refer to anyficiaries when both beneficiaries and maleficiaries are in scope, and beneficiaries or maleficiaries when one sense is apt.

Beneficiaries and maleficiaries are the broadest subarenas for anyficiaries. More concrete sub-arenas include sponsors, clients, product owners, further stakeholders, and users (primary, secondary personas etc.). Co-products such as personas and scenarios provide a wide range of stages, sharing ideas and insights with a range of audiences

Actors in this arena have similar disciplinary origins. Approaches and resources for the beneficiaries design arena mostly have origins in the human sciences (e.g., ethnography, task models and analysis, contextual inquiry), but there have also been contributions from software design and innovation (e.g., personas, empathy maps). Some approaches to scenarios draw on critical humanities practices.

## 4.3    DESIGN PARADIGMS AS ABSTRACT DESIGN SITUATIONS

The Preface drew attention to three value systems: creative design, engineering, and project management. Löwgren (1995) considered the first two. Engineering design:

> *"assumes that the 'problem' to be solved is comprehensively and precisely described, preferably in the form of a requirements specification. The mission … is to find a solution. Engineering design work is … seen as a chain of transformations from the abstract"*

Creative design:

> *is about understanding the problem as much as the resulting artifact. Creative design work is seen as a tight interplay between problem setting and problem solving. In this interplay, the design space is explored through the creation of many parallel ideas and concepts. The given assumptions regarding the problem are questioned on all levels. Creative design work is inherently unpredictable. Hence, the designer plays a personal role in the process.*

This also corresponds to Dorst and Dijkhuis' (1995) *reflection-in-action* paradigm, Lawson's (1980) *solution-focused design*, and Fallman's (2003) *romantic* or *pragmatic* accounts of design. Engineering and management combine in RILED, corresponding to Dorst and Dijkhuis' *rational problem-solving paradigm*, Lawson's (1980) *problem-focused design*, and Fallman's *conservative* account.

In Chapters 2 and 3, we saw how RILED's vocabulary outreaches conservative engineering accounts to distort presentation of rival design paradigms. In this section, we test whether ADS, as fields of interconnected design arenas, can model existing design paradigms in ways that reveal their strengths and weaknesses.

High-level differences in design have been referred to as *accounts* (Fallman) and *paradigms* (Dorst and Dijkhuis). As with "arena," the word "paradigm" has been used at different levels of abstraction in design work, from the highest-level value systems (Dorst and Dijkhuis, 1995) to Petroski's (1994) focus on specific patterns of engineering design failures. To distinguish from other uses, we can use *design work paradigm*, but having been clear, we sometimes omit "work" below, following Dorst and Dijkhuis.

Existing high-level distinctions between design practices and their underlying values do not correspond one-to-one with accounts. Creative design can correspond to Fallman's romantic or pragmatic accounts, or a mix of both. To cover both, we associate the millennia old paradigm with applied arts academies and their creative design values and practices (Chapter 2). Educational institutions in design lead their disciplines in the way that scientific institutions do for other paradigms.

The second centuries old Engineering paradigm is rooted in scientific technical and management values and practices (Chapter 3). The decades old HCD had initial roots in engineering, but its dominant human science values reduced respect for design-led practices in ways that distanced it from engineering. HCD has become sufficiently distinct to treat it as separate paradigm.

This gives us three design paradigms. With a basis for distinguishing between paradigms (Cockton, 2013b), we could show that there are others. Just as Löwgren's (1995) contrasts of engineering and creative design are "overgeneralized" and "idealised," so the three major design paradigms below should be thought of as Weberian Ideal Types, i.e., hypothetical constructs that abstract over concrete design situations. They have not been systematically validated empirically against 'all' existing design practices, but are nevertheless evidenced in established practice. While not immune to falsification, but their main value is critical, as evidenced below.

### 4.3.1    THE APPLIED ARTS DESIGN PARADIGM

Figure 4.1 shows the Applied Arts paradigm as an ADS. Three design arenas are present, but purpose and evaluation are fused in a cocktail of designers' intent (solid lines) and judgement (dashed "backtalk" lines). As in Fallman's (2003) romantic account of design, the designer is at the centre, indicated by the bold edge of the fused upper arenas. Where paradigms have centres, this reflects their dominant discipline's value commitments. Centres are power centres.

Connections between designers and artefacts are tacit, within an undifferentiated *concourse* (light-blue cloud), an open space where (unmarked) paths meet. Concourses are the circulation spaces in a multi-arena stadium. They should not be seen as a source of romantic weakness in design. Ideas, insights, and inspirations may span design arenas from the outset, so work can begin within a concourse, realising explicit elements in arenas as and when necessary. Chapter 4 (Cockton, 2020b) covers these concourse connections. They are well known in design research, but have several forms and names such as frames, partis, patterns, and primary generators. They are the one example of true "intertwining" in design work where connections arrive first and arenas must be unravelled.

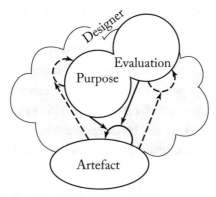

Figure 4.1: The Applied Arts Design Paradigms as an ADS.

Dashed arrows across concourses are forms of tacit connections (paths) across them. Solid arrows are explicit connections Loops indicate changes to an arena and are connected from the change's origins. Rather than a simple RILED arrow, this is a *grafted* connection, a connection to a connection. The concourse concept captures the unpredictable tacit reflective nature of creative design. Concourses are more like plates than links. They form an indivisible juncture between design arenas. They have considerable creative value, since they effortlessly bring design arenas together with no need for detailed links.

Value commitments in this paradigm include craft expertise and critical judgement. Contemporary strategic design (Stevens and Moultrie, 2011) acknowledges, values, and develops both. Thus, in the Autodesk example of an experience design alliance, designers are expected "to take responsibility for their own success in the organization" (Convertino and Fishberg, 2020). While this may feel like Fallman's (2003) romantic account, it is closer to his pragmatic one.

Design requires an artefact arena. As well as being the locus of resources and responsibilities associated with craft expertise in the applied arts, the designer is there as the fusion of evaluation and purpose, which are both clearly present from research into creative design.

There is no beneficiaries arena in the applied arts because there are no separate actors or resources to form one. How beneficiaries are considered is down to the designer. A human focus based on research into beneficiaries is optional. However, Fallman's pragmatic account can include any possible focus within applied arts. There has been a strong documented human focus in architecture since at least 80 AD (*Vitruvius' de Architectura*). A similar focus became explicit in 1950s' product design (Drefyus, 1955), three decades before HCI and IxD. Human considerations in applied arts precede HCI's HCD by millennia and still evolve separately from it (e.g., Krippendorf, 2005). Even so, the lack of an explicit beneficiaries design arena with appropriate disciplinary resources and associated actors and responsibilities differentiates applied arts from HCD.

Renn's social arena theory thus provides a useful basis for reasoning about the presence of an arena in a design paradigm. An arena's existence and degree of influence is determined by resource availability, so there must be specific resources associated with arenas in a paradigm. These can come from actors primarily associated with an arena, who will bring both tacit and explicit knowledge and other resources. A test for the presence of relevant resources is thus enough to determine the presence of an arena. A secondary check for overlooked actors can confirm or disprove an arena's absence. Without relevant actors, there can be no responsibilities and no stage (and thus no audience). Rules must apply to something, typically resources, so they too indirectly indicate an arena's presence. Connections can be argued to be present on the same basis as design arenas (associated actors or resources). Also, the lack of an arena implies the absence of all connections involving it.

Table 4.1: Comparing scientific method and engineering design for school science fair projects (Science Buddies, No Date)

| The Scientific Method | The Engineering Design Process |
|---|---|
| State your question | Define the problem |
| Do background research ||
| Formulate your hypothesis, identify variables | Specify requirements |
| Design experiment, establish procedure | Create alternative solutions, choose the best one and develop it |
| Test your hypothesis by doing an experiment | Build a prototype |
| Analyze your results and draw conclusions | Test and redesign as necessary |
| Communicate results ||

## 4.3.2   THE ENGINEERING DESIGN PARADIGM

Engineering Design is often characterized as the optimal solution of well-specified problems. Both engineering and (project) management values are involved. Its design inputs draw much more on secondary scientific knowledge than on primary contextual research. Engineering design is often closely related to "the" scientific method, with requirements specifications replacing hypotheses, and the design process replacing experimental confirmation (e.g., Table 4.1). In scientific experiments, it should be clear whether a hypothesis is confirmed or not. Similarly, in Engineering Design, it should be clear whether a design meets specified requirements or not.

Dym's (1994) "systematic, intelligent generation and evaluation of specifications for artefacts" captures the value commitments for this paradigm. Its keystone of technical requirements specification (as its purpose arena) expresses both what is to be made and how it should be evaluated. This centres Engineering Design on the artefact arena, which is thus bold in Figure 4.2. Clear relationships are meant to hold between process phases, so these are indicated as large one-way arrows, rather than a concourse as in Figure 4.1. Following Dym et al. (2014), there is no backtracking in Figure 4.2. Work on specific resources happens within design arenas, feeding resources that act as boundary objects into the next phase.

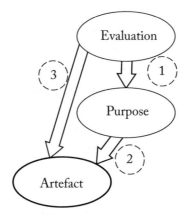

Figure 4.2: The Engineering Design Paradigm as an ADS.

Numbers alongside arrows show a preferred order for activities after requirements are specified. First, evaluation criteria are derived. Second, the artefact is designed. Third, it is verified. The first two steps could be swapped (see Figure 5.2), but it is worth establishing verification criteria before beginning a design (Cockton, 2005). Although final artefacts are implemented after an engineering design process, they are not wholly symbolic like Kitschelt's (1980) arenas, as co-products (specifications, sketches) have material forms, as do prototypes and models (Stansfield, 1976).

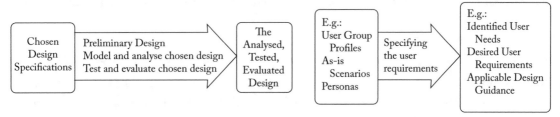

Figure 4.3: Representing phases and boundary resources, from Dym et al. (2014).

Dym et al.'s (2014) process diagram (their Figure 2.1) places phases and their tasks in round-cornered rectangles in between two arrows, one from and one to round-ended rectangles containing boundary objects from the previous phase and to the next (Figure 3.3). A simpler representation can group resources within milestone rectangles connected by transformational phase arrows. Figure 4.3 left shows a simplified fragment of Figure 2.1. A similar ISO9241-210 fragment is shown to the right. The arrows make sense as transformations, i.e., they represent work activities and not enigmatic transitions between them. Similarly, rectangles group concrete resources. However, such a representation only works for sequential processes. The ADS format is used in Figure 4.2. to allow comparisons across all design work paradigms, and to support merging them. Sequence numbers are thus needed in Figures 4.2 and 4.4.

As in the applied arts paradigm, there is no beneficiaries arena, as no specialist resources or associated actors are associated with it. User interviews are associated with the purpose arena (Dym et al., 2014) and are carried out by the same engineers who draw up requirements specifications, develop designs, compare them, and verify them. Research on beneficiaries is optional in engineering design and may well be much less present than in applied arts, leaving responsibilities here to marketing colleagues with limited engagement in detailed design.

An artefact arena must exist in any design paradigm. The other two arenas exist here because there are clear distinct engineering resources in the purpose and evaluation arenas. An example for the former is a requirements specification, and for the latter an analysis method. Distinct resources create separate purpose and evaluation arenas, unlike the applied arts paradigm.

Requirements specifications create a similar process structure to Polya's model for mathematical proof (Gedenryd, 1998), which places a plan between analysis and synthesis. As this works for tame problems, there is pressure to tame problems very early in a process ("fuzzy front end" expresses engineering values well). Parnas and Clements (1986) clearly knew the wicked nature of many software design problems (but cite no supporting empirical research). However, their response was to fake tame problems, since if "we are going to specify a standard process it seems reasonable that it should be a rational one." Given their acknowledged reality of co-evolution, a rational process has to be faked post-hoc to fake a requirements specification. Interestingly, the main difference between RILED and agile/design thinking methodologies is the lack of 'big upfront' requirements.

### 4.3.3   THE HUMAN-CENTRED DESIGN PARADIGM

The third and youngest design paradigm originally sought to extend engineering design with human-centred concerns, but at the expense of some engineering values. HCD is primarily research-driven (Gould and Lewis, 1985). The main value commitment in this paradigm is to information.

Figure 4.4 shows the HCD design paradigm. Its striking differences from the ISO 9241-210 process (Figure 3.2) must be justified. First, the purpose design arena is missing. This is because ISO 9241-210's example outputs from its requirements phase (Figure 4.3) are more closely associated with other design arenas: "identified user needs" and "desired user requirements" with the beneficiaries arena, and "applicable design guidance" with the artefact design arena. "Desired user requirements" is puzzling. If all *desired* user requirements become requirements, then "desired" is superfluous. If all *user* requirements become requirements, then "user" is superfluous. If not, for either or both, what happens in the design phase to decide which are adopted? Where do other

requirements come from, such as business, security, internal software quality, and technical requirements? The HCD process in ISO 9241-210 is incomplete, unlike the previous two paradigms. The
purpose design arena is barely present at best, and at worst does not exist because there are no
specific documented HCD resources in widespread use.

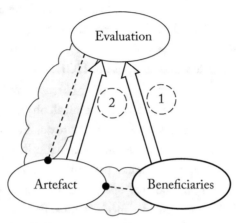

Figure 4.4: HCD paradigm as an ADS.

Only two connections can be claimed for ISO 9241-210: (1) recruitment of appropriate users
for evaluation, based on user group profiles and personas; and (2) artefacts for evaluation, including
lo-fi and hi-fi prototypes. Other connections are less clear, hence the use of two concourse clouds
with two dotted problematic connections: implications for design (bottom, Dourish, 2006) and
downstream utility (left, Law, 2006). Such connections must exist, but the HCI literature has problems with both. Even when participative design involves beneficiaries in design and evaluation, it
is not clear if participants are amateur designers within an applied arts paradigm, or HCD workers
who transform their own insights into design proposals.

Concourses apart, connections can only exist when connected arenas are sufficiently developed to connect to them. There can be few implications for design of an artefact that does not yet
exist. Implications are always for a design, so both artefacts and beneficiaries must be far enough
advanced to see implications. An arena that has not yet been advanced at all, such as later phases in
first iterations of RILED processes, cannot be connected to because there is nothing to interface to.

The large arrows show two confident connections. User research results in boundary resources (user profiles and personas) at the interface of the beneficiaries arena, which can be used to
recruit evaluation participants, who bring further resources to evaluation (e.g., documents they are
working on for evaluating office productivity software). This arrow is not a mathematical function,
but the domain (beneficiaries resources) and range (evaluation resources) are clear.

It is not clear how a purpose arena could function in HCD. If only user needs can guide
design, then no intermediate requirements are needed. Instead, new knowledge on project stake-

holders (especially target users), project goals, and usage settings would be gathered before any consideration of artefact features and qualities, and then continuously refreshed, particularly by evaluations. HCD expects designers to prioritise user needs and preferences over their own expertise and judgement, or even eliminate the latter (Gould and Lewis, 1985). HCD thus centres on beneficiaries (bold edged oval in Figure 4.4). There has been a shift here, even in the relatively short life span of HCD. The Star Life Cycle, based on some rare research into design within HCI, placed evaluation at the centre of HCD (Hartson and Hix, 1989). This centre may have shifted as a result of a lack of connections to evaluation from purpose in HCD.

HCD evolved from Human Factors Engineering (*Ergonomics* in Europe) after World War II. For almost three decades, it mostly focused on anatomical, physiological, motor, and perceptual factors. Often, ergonomists were engineers with postgraduate qualifications, enabling effective work in engineering contexts. Human Factors Engineering systematically explores the impact of specific biological and psychological parameters on human performance and comfort. Human performance requirements could be included in engineering specifications and verified as part of testing, and were the bases for 1980s usability requirements specifications. Experiences with usability specifications were mixed, so HCD groups at Digital and IBM focused instead on contextual understanding (Whiteside et al., 1988), separating HCD from its human factors roots. An embryonic purpose arena was lost, the beneficiaries arena moved to the centre of HCD, and a second wave HCI (Rogers et al., 1993) drove a disciplinary wedge between the evaluation (psychology) and beneficiaries (ethnography) design arenas (Siegel and Dray, 2005).

Without specifications, it was no longer clear what usability evaluation should assess (Cockton, 2007a), nor could contextual research provide scientifically derived performance targets or feature specifications (e.g., reach distance, display brightness, keycap size). Without these, IxD decisions connected poorly with user research and usage evaluation. HCD was no longer engineering, but a separate adjunct paradigm addressing only some design matters. In ISO 9241-210, planning only includes HCD. There is no product strategy or programme roadmap, no operational support for products in the market, and no asynchronous out-of-process opportunities such as trade show demonstrations.

### 4.3.4   COMPARING DESIGN PARADIGMS

The three design paradigms may be ideal types, but have falsifiable positions based on resources or actors, and can roughly identify strengths and weaknesses. The strength of the applied arts paradigm is also its main weakness, its centre, i.e., the exploitation of designers' craft expertise and aesthetic and critical judgement. The strength of engineering design lies in precise problem specifications that focus design on solutions while also directing how these will be evaluated. Its weakness is that its centre, the artefact, must be specified completely in advance, along with its evaluation criteria. It is best suited for tame problems (Rittel and Webber, 1973) because a wicked problem "is not understood until after the formulation of a solution" (Conklin, 2005). When engineering design strives to exit its "fuzzy front end" at the earliest opportunity, weak understandings of wicked problems result. Simon's (1969) "science of design … can only be applied only to well-formed problems extracted from situations of practice" (Schön, 1983).

HCD's strength is its ability to involve its centre, i.e., beneficiaries, early and late in a process. Its weakness is its limited support for detailed design and implementation. Both engineering and HCD are single artefact methodologies, whereas applied arts can support a complete design programme (e.g., a fashion collection, physical storage system, dinner services, cloud services roadmap, or mobile phone range).

Strengths and weaknesses follow from different emphases and foci within each paradigm, reinforced by differences in disciplinary vocabularies, e.g., engineering design's *problems* vs. applied arts' *design briefs*. The artefact arena is always present in design paradigms, but the absence or blurring of others indicates lack of value commitments. There will be some ephemeral or tacit considerations of missing arenas and connections, as indicated by concourses and dotted connections, but these will not be well supported.

Design purpose can be tacit and largely experimental in applied arts, with creative insights and technical opportunities shaping artefact evolution. Such craft practices lie at one extreme of applied arts. At the other, purpose in commercial design (product, fashion marketing, retail interiors, etc.) aligns closely to business needs via clearly expressed positive value propositions. In contrast, HCD can be unclear on choices about purpose beyond generics such as satisfaction and ease of use and learning.

Evaluation, too, differs across paradigms. Engineering has a strong focus on evaluation of the designed artefact, rather than its resulting usage. HCD has an uneasy relationship with the artefact, but has lavished attention on empirical evaluation. HCD and Engineering evaluation activities are typically explicit, distinct, and planned, with expectations for design modifications in response to unsatisfactory results. In contrast, applied arts evaluation is often tacit, opportunistic, and unscheduled, and can focus as much on motivating purposes as on their achievement. Reflection by designers can result in changes of purpose, changes to artefacts, or both. Whereas the artefact and intended purpose blur in Engineering Design, evaluation and purpose blur in the applied arts. This holds for the distinct practices of the "crit" (*critique*, especially in design education). Crits do not just focus on aesthetic qualities. Purpose is often more in focus, i.e., is that design worthwhile? This extends from design school crits to the wider world of awards, juried exhibitions, and critical reviews. There is an explicit paradigmatic choice within applied arts to not direct evaluation, but to instead trust designers' judgements on whether to stick with current artefact features and qualities, to choose new ones, or to revise design intentions.

Much of HCD's initial success and attractiveness can be attributed to its evaluative focus on usage. Such practices are largely absent in other paradigms. However, HCD evaluators often choose evaluation criteria independently of design strategy, especially generic metrics such as ease of learning, time on task, error rates, contextual fit or subjective satisfaction (Cockton, 2007a).

Each paradigm has different forms of evaluation: testing, assessment, verification, validation, and critique. Beneficiaries also differ, with stakeholders (including users) receive varying attention. HCD may not have existed if other paradigms had an effective focus on stakeholders. However, HCD is inconsistent on whether it is human-centred for all beneficiaries, or mostly user-focused. Human factors engineering focuses on universal re-usable parameters more than individual differences.

| Table 4.2: Relative strengths and weakness of each design paradigm | | | | |
|---|---|---|---|---|
| | **Artefact** | **Purpose** | **Evaluations** | **Beneficiaries** |
| **Applied Arts** | 👍 | 👍 | 👎 | 👎 |
| **Engineering** | 👍 | 👎 | 👍 | 👎 |
| **Human-centred** | 👎 | 👎 | 👍 | 👍 |

Design paradigms have different relative strengths and weaknesses in terms of the relative presence or absence of design arenas within their scope (Table 4.2). This is reflected in differing constructions of success, i.e., applied arts seeks to demonstrate craft excellence, engineering aims to achieve required properties, and HCD aims to meet user needs. Design thus succeeds when:

- requirements are satisfied (engineering);

- designers are satisfied (applied arts, design-led); and

- others are satisfied (HCD).

When there is no separate purpose arena, its scope is absorbed into a paradigm's centre, which functions as a black hole in this respect. With such distinct scopes, success criteria, connections, and centres (Figures 4.1, 4.2, and 4.4), work within each paradigm often can be misunderstood and mistrusted from the perspectives of others. Each has something to offer, but also has weaknesses. None are adequate for excellence in 21st-century design. There is an opportunity to merge the three paradigms into a more comprehensive one.

## 4.3.5   FAIRNESS FOR DESIGN ARENAS FROM DESIGN PARADIGMS

Renn (1992) argues that his social arena theory can be a model for fairness and competence. The brief analyses above have applied social arena concepts to each design arena. A basis here for a fair approach to design arenas moves beyond the favourite centres of major design paradigms that deliver on narrow value commitments. Each major design paradigm omits, merges or restrains design arenas. Viewed from above, from a meta-design perspective, this is not justified. We need to accommodate all four design arenas with appropriate balance and scope, taking note of the differences between created and curated arenas.

"Design creates the spaces in which it operates" (Gaver, 2011). *Created* arenas have limited or no existence before projects, and must be specifically designed. Both a_tefacts and evaluations are designed rather than selected, unlike *curated* arenas: purpose and anyficiaries are judicious selections and interpretations from external human realities. Design teams curate by selecting, interpreting, and communicating who matters, what matters about them, and what could matter to them: design thus creates *and* curates the spaces in which it operates. Dorst (2015) sees his fields as being created, but by connecting anyficiaries to purpose, curation better indicates grounding in external realities.

*Persistent* arenas (artefacts and anyficiaries) outlive projects. Artefacts are deployed or used by beneficiaries. *Ephemeral* arenas (antefacts, purpose, and evaluation) may not outlive projects. All intended purpose is not achieved all of the time by deployed artefacts, but unintended value can result from appropriation (Von Hipple, 1986). However, co-products from ephemeral arenas may persist within design programmes, especially when they support strategic design alliances within an organisation. Such alliances need patience, persistence, and impactful collaboration (Convertino and Fishberg, 2020). Re-use and wider adoption of resulting co-products provides worth to alliances, supporting individual growth, learning, betterment, and impact with organisations.

The above analysis of design arenas provides insights into the strengths and weaknesses of the three major design paradigms. A post-centric comprehensive approach to design work paradigms should be part of our response. Design centres are power centres that predetermine inclusion, resources and processes. Such predetermination is at odds with the realities of creative design work. However, any new paradigm would also be prone to structural imperialism, when what we need is sufficient structural indeterminacy (Renn, 1992) to make room for a broad range of design practices, including ones that do not as yet exist.

Beck (1992) argued that we have left behind modernism, but few still fully embrace postmodernism. Instead, our current state is one of reflexive modernization, a *post paradigmatic* culture with both modern and postmodern elements. This radicalised modernity neither accepts objectification and a scientific monopoly on rationality (the dogma of Scientism), nor expects clear demarcations between solutions and causes of problems. We have already rejected the latter and embraced an alternative design rationality that combines creation and curation to avoid relativism through tests against realities (Renn, 1992).

## 4.4    A POST-CENTRIC ABSTRACT DESIGN SITUATION TEMPLATE

The section proposes a new post-centric template for design work. It can be made more concrete in a variety of ways, including cutting back to an existing major design paradigm. Its intended use, however, is to direct design organisations to form new design paradigms that are *radicalised* in Beck's (1992) sense. The template is *post paradigmatic*, mixing elements of existing paradigms in a radicalised modernity.

Incorrect beliefs about design have constrained critical creative design practices. Five decades of research into design have shown how wrong most widely held beliefs are. We must move on. Figure 4.5 diagrammatically indicates a post-centric fusion of the three major design paradigms, with a comprehensive span of connections between arenas. There is only one arrow (grafted) connection, the rest are deliberately fuzzy tracks. No arena has a bold edge because success cannot be solely a function of one centre arena. Instead, *multifocal* episodes move design work forward.

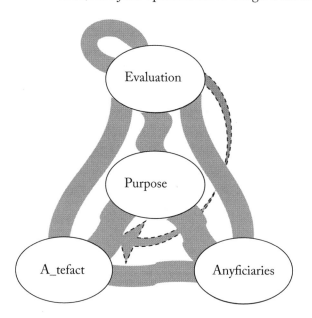

Figure 4.5: A broad post-centric ADS template for BIG design.

The BIG ADS template responds to Wolf et al.'s (2006) argument that superficial disciplinary conflicts are surmountable and that caricatures can be overcome. Wolf et al.'s "creative symbiosis with HCD" is given an explicit template structure in Figure 4.5. HCD is too limited to ever survive on its own. It needs engineering, creative design, or both to have a_tefacts to evaluate. Both HCD practice areas (anyficiaries, evaluation) can be very valuable, but only when tightly coupled to other arenas, e.g., evaluation to purpose, and anyficiaries via usage of a_tefacts to purpose. While "interaction between people and things" (Poggenpohl, 2017) is not HCD's sole preserve, HCD has a stronger grasp on it than the other paradigms.

There are key points of contact with Fallman's (2003) pragmatic account of design, which do not align well with any existing paradigm:

- design arenas "cram" specific design situations: artefacts and beneficiaries (people and practices) bring "histories, identities, goals, and plans" from associated disciplinary and professional practices;

- the *purpose* design arena is central to Fallman's "creation of meaning";

- the *evaluation* design arena can be part of his "hermeneutic process of interpretation"; and

- *connections* between design arenas are formed as "designers iteratively interpret the effects of their designs on the situation at hand."

Fallman's pragmatic account can accommodate his other two accounts, but the reverse is not true. Disciplinary and professional practices associated with design arenas preserve conservative and romantic accounts. Both anyficiaries and evaluation are home to (conservative) scientific practices. The a_tefact arena is home to (romantic) designerly practices of inventiveness. Similarly, purpose is home to (romantic) generosity. The lack of an equivalent existing paradigm for Fallman's *pragmatic* account is an opportunity to form new ones from a *template*.

New design paradigms can be formed from the template by committing to the four design arenas and connections between them. Design arenas can be changed as long as Heskett's (2005) means, ends, beneficiaries, and evaluations remain covered. The template can be used in two steps. First design arenas are selected, adapted, or added, along with connection structures to form an ADS. Secondly, the ADS is assessed for its ability to support BIG design progression.

The template fills gaps in existing design paradigms, raising the question as to whether lacunation (gap forming) is still possible. One basis for lacunation is to identify missing design arenas. The four in Figure 4.5 are derived from Heskett's (2005) enumeration of the choices leading to design outcomes, which is broader than typical definitions of design (Cockton, 2010a). No new design arena has been identified for over a decade. A black swan here is logically possible, but unlikely.

Another basis for lacunation is missing connections. Figure 4.5 only shows some examples:

- binary connections in both directions between all pairs of arenas;

- one loop from evaluation back to itself; and

- a grafted connection from evaluation to the usage connection between purpose and a_tefact (when we evaluate usage, we evaluate a connection, not isolated design arenas).

There are substantially more possible connections beyond those in Figure 4.5, which while broader than existing design paradigms are still simplified. Questions thus arise as to which connections are missing, and whether they have any practical consequence. We can use the concept of *arity* from mathematics in an analysis here. Arity counts parameters for functions, but we can extend it to count connected arenas. Connections can be unary (loops), binary (between two arenas), ternary (between 3) or quaternary (4). With 4 design arenas, the maximum possibilities for each are 4 for unary, 18 for binary (6 concourses and 6 pairs in two directions each), and dozens for ternary and quaternary connections. George (2016) introduced loops. With concourses, this increases the connection count in Cockton (2010a). However, the scores of connections here are just a start. Adding grafted connections (and connections to connections to connections etc.) spawn infinite connections.

There is no theoretical basis for ruling out lacunation by checking for every possible connection, since these are infinite. An ADS template can thus be (very) comprehensive, but never theoretically complete. Much combinatorial complexity arises from only four design arenas (and their many subarenas), adding credibility to Davies and Talbot's (1987) descriptions of elite designers' imago moments. How can it be that "everything eventually connects" (Eames) except subconsciously? Interestingly, the word "sketch" originates in the Greek *skhedios*, something without preparation.

Working concurrently on design arenas and interconnections creates extensive dynamic potential. Cockton (2010a) relates this to the philosopher Alain Badiou's *situational ontology*, which unifies objects and relations. Design situations can be highly unstable. Moves in one arena can trigger a chain of events (i.e., arena changes, new connections). Such shifts or design moves are not scripted by a fixed process, but instead match Dorst's (2015) observations of frames as inspiring, provoking, captivating, inspiring, uniting, evoking, eliciting, and being shared. A good frame for one arena creates good potentials to connect with others. In Badiou's terms, "framing can be an event." There will always be adventitious aspects of design.

The ADS template in Figure 4.5 is compatible with Chapter 2's three key realities of creative design. All design arenas, however conceived, can co-evolve in any order, producing backtalk within and between them. Progress can be assessed through reflection *in* and *on* action and adjusted through reflection *for* action (Killion and Todnem, 1991). Generosity depends on practices within a separate purpose arena and its integration with other arenas (Cockton, 2020b, Chapters 2 and 4). This creates a better position for generous design than any of the three major paradigms. Our new post-paradigmatic ADS is thus a template for more concrete and focused paradigms that can all be BIG, i.e.,

- *balanced* across design arenas;

- *integrated* across design arenas; and

- *generous* in the extent of a resulting Axiofact's worth (see the section that follows).

Generosity can be achieved without an explicit purpose arena with a Wo-Fo, as seen in design history examples such as Ken Clarke's sewing machine redesign (Chapter 2). However, we argue in this book that an explicit Wo-Fo (Cockton, 2020b, Chapter 2) encourages a multidisciplinary design team's generosity through integrating design arenas to be generous (Cockton, 2020b, Chapter 4), while drawing on an appropriate balance of *memoranda* (Cockton, 2020b, Chapter 3), as explained next.

### 4.4.1 AXIOFACTS AND THE LIMITATIONS OF DORST'S LOGICAL FRAMES

1960s design methodology and its aftermath sought rational planning and control, despite adventitious moves in creative design work. A more realistic approach is to post-rationalise design work through reflection in, on, and for action. Each episode of creatively led design work comes to a close with a pause for reflection. Such post-rationalisation is much like the honing of a mathematical proof, which Gedenryd (1998) argues does not follow Polya's (1945) prescribed order of analysis-plan-synthesis. There are thus no numbers on arrows in Figure 4.5. They have no place in a meta-design model that aims to subsume and extend existing design work paradigms. Co-evolution of arenas makes prediction of work orders impossible. Progressions do not follow a process. However, given the grip of RILED language, logical orders can even entrap expert design theorists who argue against RILED's control mentality.

We see this in Dorst's (2015) derivation of frames, which begins with comparisons of four forms of logic: deduction, induction, normal abduction, and design abduction. Dorst models each form of logic with three separate variables in an identical structure:

WHAT + HOW leads to OUTCOME

- The WHAT variable spans elements of the world, people, and things, a concourse connection across a_tefact and anyficiaries.

- The HOW variable connects these elements in patterns of relationships that lead to ...

- The OUTCOME variable, a concourse of achieved purpose across evaluation and purpose.

Each form of logic has two knowns and one unknown, except design abduction, which has two unknowns. In deduction, the HOW and the WHAT are known and the unknown OUTCOME is deduced from them. In induction, the OUTCOME and the WHAT are known and the HOW is induced from them. In abduction, the OUTCOME and the HOW are known and the WHAT is identified through a problem-solving process. In design abduction, only the OUTCOME is known and both the WHAT and the HOW are formed in a double creative step that involves much learning and experimentation. However, despite its name, Dorst does not intend to privilege this basic pattern of reasoning. All four forms of logic occur in design work. The first three are not problematic as they largely support specific activities *within* design arenas. The difficult co-evolution of connected design arenas is left to design abduction, which has limitations in this regard.

A framework with binary knowns/unknowns inevitably imposes a sequenced process. The knowns are fully known before unknowns are considered, imposing a temporal structure like analysis-synthesis. Dorst's equation like structure does provide "enough conceptual tools" to analyse the four basic reasoning patterns, but it imposes too much on design work. Wicked problems tell us that the OUTCOME (purpose arena) is unlikely to be fully known first, nor can achieved purpose be evaluated without a WHAT and HOW to produce phenomena to observe. Relationships between WHAT, HOW, and OUTCOME require all to be at least partially in place for WHAT+ HOW to observably lead to OUTCOME. They must co-evolve. We need an alternative to Dorst's logic-based frames and their residual RILED ordering.

Dorst (2015) uses two further senses of frame, a "slippery" notion "completely defined by its use." In one of his five lessons from design (Section 2.1.3), he sketches a pragmatic form of frame that aligns with research: a *set of relationships that can be given coherence by a metaphor*. It often involves themes (Section 2.1.4). Coherence across themes is important and points to the need for a simpler structure than the potentially infinite connections that can be built from Figure 4.5. However, he also defines a frame logically as *HOW leads to OUTCOME*. Design abduction is reduced to general abduction once HOW is instantiated. This "logical" form of frame shows how "by applying a particular pattern of relationships we can create a desired outcome."

Darke's (1979) primary generators are broader than Dorst's logical frames, as they can combine some of a WHAT, HOW, and OUTCOME. Dorst's "pattern of relationships" is hypothetical, and thus achievable outcomes can only be conjectural. It is hard to see how this testing is possible without instantiating one or more WHATs.

Dorst derives his first form of frame from a framework of logic and reasoning patterns, and his second from lessons from design research. For design abduction he moves to two variables when he should have moved to three. These variables are not instantiated in separate single moves, but instead are progressively instantiated during multiple episodes of design work. Within each episode, WHAT elements (a_tefacts, anyficiaries) can be instantiated at different rates, and also put aside. The same applies to OUTCOME (as evaluated purpose) and HOW (as patterns of connections). There is a risk that the technically minded will not read beyond the formulaic logical version of a frame and take less notice (or none) of the pragmatic account 10 pages later.

The ADS in Figure 4.5 is closely aligned with Dorst's pragmatic frames but not his logical ones. The latter are more constrained than Figure 4.5's post-centric model, which gives this formula:

$$A\_tefact \otimes Memoranda \text{ progresses to } Axiofact$$

*Axio-fact* is a neologism based on "arte-fact." It is *worth* (rather than simply a thing) that has *been made* from the connections between an a_tefact and its memoranda. I have replaced the "="

in Cockton (2017) with *progresses* to: axiofacts are forged in design and then usage, not on paper. The symbol ⊗ represents the complex web of connections between an a_tefact and its *memoranda* (things to be borne in mind), the connected elements in the other design arenas. These are the "other ideas" of Davies and Talbot (1987) about self, others, and organisations. An axiofact is their "right idea" with its "certainty of knowledge of something worthwhile" and "the chance of favourable prospects to response with some risk" (Davies and Talbot, 1987). A right idea can thus be understood as plausibly demonstrably worthwhile (like Dorst's logical frames). THE idea, their right idea, is an idea about implementing other ideas. It is not the simple isolated original idea of much creativity research. Nor are the connections simply Koestler's creative *bisociation* (1964), where only two previously unrelated areas blend together. THE idea involves Dorst's WHAT as much as his HOW or OUTCOME.

An axiofact involves multiple frames, not just Dorst's single "HOW leads to OUTCOME." First, each design arena is framed. Second, several further frames give coherence to complex webs of connections. Frames thus extend to all design arenas and their integrating connections.

Elements from multiple subarenas can be integrated through many different forms of connection. There is a massive gap between simple accounts of "creativity" and the actual complexity of design work as revealed by empirical studies and deepened by theoretical analyses. At the same time, the four design arenas are more concrete than Poggenpohl's (2017) "qualitative work in many dimensions."

Connections and their "indexical character" show how a design is "new and valuable, rather than leaving the artefact to speak for itself—as if it could" (Gaver and Bowers, 2012). This is why the true outcome of design is neither artefacts nor co-products, but axiofacts, both in practice and research. By connecting with a_tefacts, themes become memoranda. Until then, they hang in the balance, neither positive nor negative, until they connect in new ways, offering bases for portfolio annotation (Gaver and Bowers, 2012).

Axiofacts are a basis for a new *science of the worthwhile*. A science of the artificial (Simon, 1969) is not enough because artefacts are not enough. Axiofacts deliver on designers' responsibility to humanise technology (Poggenpohl, 2017) rather "merely designing something." Axiofacts contribute in a meaningful way through opportunities and obligations (Junginger, 2017).

Connections within axiofacts, like design arenas, are created or curated, not simply discovered. Fallman (2003) borrows Schön's (1983) vocabulary to characterise design as "unfolding a coherent whole—a previously nonexistent artifact—from the various bits and pieces gathered in the process of research, but which simply put together do not by themselves form the whole." However, "unfolding," like "emergence," suggests a complete pre-existing hidden structure (over and above "the various bits and pieces gathered") that designers simply unfold to reveal and discover. Even in the hands of a philosophically adept writer such as Schön, language can bring connotations that must be exposed and critiqued. As a creative designer, Gaver (2011) is clear: "design creates the spaces in which it operates." There is nothing to unfold. Everything is progressively formed, revised, or retired. There is no nomad's carpet to unfold, nor is there an oak waiting to emerge from an acorn. Design weaves together wishes with the adventitious. There is intent but the progression of design work is unpredictable. Design is a cocktail of expertise, adventure and the adventitious.

Section 4.2 considered design arenas through the lens of Renn's (1992) social arena theory. Section 4.3 modelled three major design paradigms using ADS structures. This section has shown how connected design arenas can instantiate a post-centric ADS template from which a range of novel BIG design paradigms can derived. Balance is achieved by appropriate effort across design arenas, and generosity through multiple perspectives on purpose. Integration is achieved by connections. BIG is true to the etymology of paradigm: showing side-by-side (so that patterns may be seen). BIG paradigms show design arenas side by side, opening up conversations about patterns of connections. The major design paradigms are "dogmadigms"; showing opinion (of what seems good). The template in Figure 4.5 can let hundreds of paradigm flowers blossom.

## 4.5    CHAPTER SUMMARY

At the end of Chapter 3, two of the questions from Chapter 1 were carried forward and four were added. These can be renumbered as follows.

1. What are the main areas of design work? Can it reasonably be divided up in some way (as in Table 1.1)? What are the alternatives to the areas in Table 1.1?

2. Are there standard progressions that can organise design work without regimenting it into a sequence of phases? How much iteration is needed? How much concurrency can be handled simultaneously? Is there a correct structure?

3. What forms and levels of abstraction would a comprehensive model of design work have?

4. What sort of connections and interfaces would be in this model?

5. What forms of tracking would a new model support?

6. What would progress look like when design work is tracked with support from a new model?

The last three questions will be addressed for the first time in the next chapter, where the worth of ADS framing of design work is extended beyond theory to practice. Current answers to the first three questions above, with cross-references to seven positions in Chapter 3's manifesto (e.g., M1) are as follows.

1. Alternative design arena names were given to Table 1.1's areas and Heskett's forms of design choice (M1). The current four design arenas appear to be sufficient and necessary. There must be an a_tefact. Without a separate purpose arena, there can be adverse consequences for evaluation (lost bases for appropriate measures and targets) and for purpose itself, which becomes absorbed into beneficiaries (identified needs, wants and pain points only) or a_tefacts (technical requirements). Chapter 2 of Book 2 (Cockton, 2020b) focuses on approaches and resources for a separate design purpose arena.

2. There is no correct progression structure, only a post-centric template is realistic, which can be specialised for specific projects, programmes and organisations. Concurrency is the norm (M2), but it is not clear at this point how much can be handled simultaneously. Figure 4.5's post-centric template does not constrain concurrency, but derived paradigms can.

3. ADS can be used to form comprehensive models of design work, Design subarenas and detailed connections reduce abstraction (M5). Chapter 5 develops increasingly concrete abstractions for tracking design work.

The complexity of design can be overstated. Arenas can be tamed by subarenas. It is connections where complexity can overwhelm. They cannot be managed by fixed upfront processes.

In relation to Manifesto position 7, we have begun to retire tired RILED concepts.

- Problems and solutions impose a linear model of design, and are replaced by memoranda (Purpose, Evaluations, and Anyficiaries) and A_tefacts, known collectively as design arenas. An arena is either created or curated, and persistent or ephemeral.

- Processes are replaced by ADS *progressions*.

- Phases (stages) are replaced by *episodes* that can focus in different ways on multiple design arenas. Episodes are coherent time spans within progressions. Coherence reflects sustained framing of one or more design arenas. When one or more arenas' frames change significantly, an episode comes to an end and the next is planned for.

- Implications for design and downstream utility are replaced by *connections for this a_tefact*.

Language matters. While STEM disciplines try to tame language with technical writing style guides, the humanities embrace the untamed powerful expressiveness of language. Restrictions on language in the name of objective value-free communication result in unavoidable lacunae that hide bias and oversights. It is important to have a lexicon for design work that is free of assumptions, bias, constraints and omissions. The next chapter and Book 2 (Cockton 2020b, Chapters 2, 3, and 4) add to this lexicon.

# CHAPTER 5

# Tracking BIG Creative Design Practice

The major design paradigms can be modelled using ADS (Figures 4.1, 4.2, and 4.4), as can a template for more comprehensive BIG design paradigms (Figure 4.5). ADS give initial direction for new design paradigms by covering all Heskett's (2005) types of design choices, with an infinite set of possible unary, binary, ternary, and quaternary connections with increasingly complex grafted connections (in theory). ADS support theoretical analyses that suggest ways to overcome limitations of existing major design work paradigms. More comprehensive paradigms can accommodate the key realities of creative design practice (Chapter 2), and also, with some compromises, engineering, management, and human-centred values and practices (Chapter 3). Creative practices must take precedence over unsubtle management control where wild (not "wicked") problems are involved. Here multi-arena design episodes replace "add-another-arena" phases of engineering design, where "completed" arenas are arrested when adding the next in sequence.

Thinking back to Chapter 1, the CloudBooks team's settled working patterns did not appear to be ideal: they had no explicit co-ordination across their work areas, nor was it clear if their balance of effort reflected available resources more than strategic need. ADS provide a basis for reasoning about ideal balance across design areas and ideal integration through connections. However, no ADS in Chapter 4 indicates balance of effort or outcomes for each arena.

Chapter 4's ADS are too abstract for most practical planning and deliberation in concrete design situations. They are MADS. They support pertinent theoretical analyses, but at project level, we must zoom in, for which George (2016) developed three further abstractions: another ADS and two for design arenas. George (2016) used multiple levels of abstraction when tracking development of *MyCareCircle*, a web-based information and social support system for care circles of children with major motor impairments, plus some additional groups with special needs.

In engineering and HCD paradigms, progress can be measured against upfront plans (Parnas and Clements, 1986). Project managers will know which phases have been completed, which boundary resources have passed between them, which phase is in progress, and what remains to be done for a current iteration. They may have some idea of what work will be carried out on the next iteration, especially with backlogs in agile development (Cockton, 2016b). In contrast, for a concurrent paradigm, design teams must know what has been completed for each arena and its connections, which arenas are driving forward the current episode, what remains to be done, and when this may be done (i.e., current or future episode). The team must be able to track, reflect on, deliberate on, and advance design work.

Gedenryd (1998) argued that need for theory in design was still great. There have been few major advances as yet. This chapter presents a novel family of theoretically grounded visual and textual records of design work at multiple scopes and levels of abstraction.

1. MADS (Figures 4.1, 4.2, 4.4, 4.5) and sequences of them

2. Proportional Abstract Design Situations (PADS)

3. Design Arena Frames (DAFs)

4. Design Arena Notes (DANs)

5. Connection Notes (CoNs)

6. Connection Frames (CoFs)

The first two representations are snapshots of a project's work. The next two only apply to design arenas. The last two focus on connections. The theoretical grounding comes from:

1. design arenas as being:

    a. distinct forms of design choice that determine design outcomes (Heskett, 2005);

    b. structurally very similar to social arenas in political science, especially as characterised by Renn (1992), but with some key differences for design work;

2. connections between design arenas as:

    a. being dynamic elements of Badiou's situational ontology (Cockton 2010a, e.g., concourse connections are close in structure to Badiou's parts);

    b. fusing existing coherence metaphors (e.g., Aalto's harmony, Davis and Talbot's imago);

    c. subsuming design research concepts such as *frames* (Dorst, 2015), *primary generators* (Darke, 1979), *bridge building* (Cross, 1997), and *synthesis* (Kolko, 2015);

    d. necessitated by co-evolution of design arenas and shaped by backtalk; and

    e. creating assemblages/assemblies/actor-networks via "careful plaiting of weak ties" and "netting, lacing, weaving, twisting of ties that are weak by themselves" (Latour, 1996).

The first four representations (George, 2016) are introduced first, followed by a few examples of their use in industry and education. The last two representations are then presented, followed by alternative representations for communicating the results of research through design. The importance of reflection and deliberation is then addressed, before this chapter and book conclude with a summary and update of progress relative to the 6 questions and 7 manifesto positions that were developed up to Chapter 3 and partially addressed in Chapter 4.

## 5.1    TRACKING DESIGN WORK WITH MADS

Chapter 4 ADS are MADS. Despite a very high abstraction level, they support interesting analyses and comparisons. Chapter 4 MADS can be extended with episode generators and by representations of progressions as sequences of MADS (SoMADS).

### 5.1.1    ADDING EPISODE GENERATORS TO MADS

In Chapter 4, bold edges on arenas indicated the centres of design work paradigms. George (2016) generalised Darke's (1979) primary generators from design inception to a complete design progression by identifying generator(s) for each design episode (Figure 5.1). These "primary generators" are renamed here to *episode generators* to distinguish them from Darke's original concept. MADS were drawn for the end of each episode in a research through design (RtD) project that tracked structure and focus (George, 2016), exposing how episode generators change. Loops are often associated with a predominant arena, with its internal logic driving design work forward.

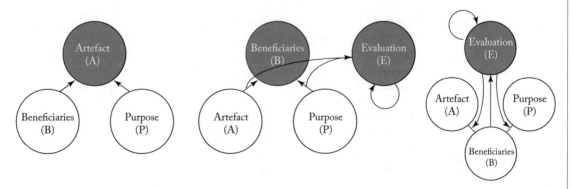

Figure 5.1: Tracking episode generators using MADS (George, 2016) before renaming of beneficiaries and artefact arenas in Cockton (2017).

The MADS start simple on the left of Figure 5.1 with a one-arena generator (shaded orange) for the second design-led episode in George's research through design. Four field work activities in this episode increasingly indicated that the initial conjectured antefact (a decision support system) would not fit its intended context.

The central MADS in Figure 5.1 is for a single activity in the fourth RtD episode: the piloting of a multi-arena questionnaire. In contrast to much HCD practice, this was not focused solely on beneficiaries, but also gathered data on intended purpose and some features of an envisaged artefact. New insights into beneficiaries were linked to purpose and the envisaged artefact, and then further to evaluation via two grafted connections. The loop, introduced by George, indicates revisions to the multi-arena questionnaire as a result of piloting. A two-arena episode generator resulted.

The right MADS is for a questionnaire fielding activity, immediately after piloting. Here, evaluation alone is the episode generator. It was focused on connections between beneficiaries and both purpose and the envisaged artefact, hence the two grafted connections. The loop represents reflection on the fielding of the questionnaire and its results.

### 5.1.2    SEQUENCES OF MADS (SOMADS)

As a deliberately atemporal construct, MADSs are snapshots that cannot represent process. Additions are needed, such as the order numbers in Figures 4.2 and 4.4, which are not easy to follow. However, a progression can be represented as a Sequence of MADS (SoMADS), revealing shifts in focus, scope, balance, and integration across episodes. A snapshot sequence can model a concurrent progression of arenas, with connections continuously formed and reformed.

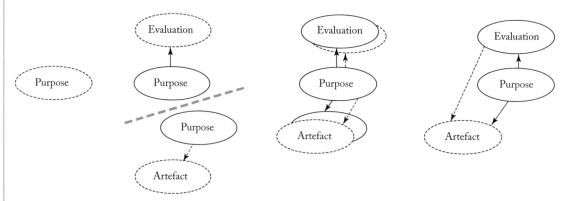

Figure 5.2: A RILED process as a SoMADS.

RILED processes are a very restricted (and risky) sequence, where each phase snapshot comprises completed and in progress design arenas and connections. Figure 5.2 shows a SoMADS for rational idealised Engineering Design (Parnas and Clements, 1986). The first episode focuses on purpose. It has a dashed outline as the new in-progress arena introduced for this phase. The next connects purpose to either the evaluation (planning) or the artefact arena, with the former preferable since knowledge of evaluation criteria can guide artefact development (Cockton, 2005). Again, dashed outlines indicate the added arena and connection for a phase. The third phase adds the arena missing from the previous one (hence alternative solid and dashed outlines), and the final phase adds a connection from evaluation to the artefact. This is visually easier to follow than order numbers and shows that, while an ADS is a status construct, it can be used to represent progression. A much more demanding (and very revealing) test is to model progression within the Frame Creation Model (FCM) for project initiation (Dorst, 2015) with a SoMADS. Figure 5.3 models eight steps of the FCM Model as ADS.

The first seven to eight steps can be covered in a two-hour initiation workshop, following "an extensive period of dialogue with external stakeholders" that prepares for the first five steps to different extents.

1. *Archaeology of the problem situation*: this is modelled as a concourse where understanding of anyficiaries informs possible design purpose (new benefits, current adverse factors).

2. *Establishing the Core Paradox*: this is modelled by adding current central and relevant artefacts to the concourse to identify paradoxes as loss of worth (desired benefits undermined by adverse consequences of current artefacts). "BECAUSE" structures are used by Dorst to expose the chains of consequences that lead to unwelcome values, which may result in a true or "semi" paradox.

3. *The Context*: there is a deliberate sharp break here where the focus returns exclusively to improving understandings of all relevant stakeholders (hence the loop).

4. Bourdieu's *Field* concept directs expansion of the problem situation context (hence the loop) by considering all potential "players" and their "currencies" as power interests, values, practices, and potential frames. Note the separation of purpose (players' values) from anyficiaries (players) in preparation for a focus on shared underlying values to develop common purpose across the field.

5. *Themes* (Section 2.1.4): as in step two, current artefacts are brought back into focus to expose current adverse consequences and important values. The latter inform the OUTCOME component of a logical frame (HOW leads to OUTCOME). A connection to purpose is grafted to the current fit between anyficiaries and artefacts (binary connection, grey fill indicates a "root stock" for grafting onto). Themes emerge from considering grafted connections, which "bridge the human (cultural) domain and the technical or economic realms" (Dorst, 2015).

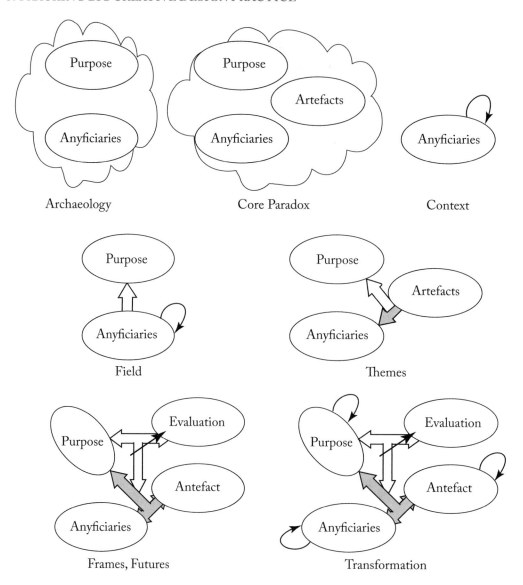

Figure 5.3: Dorst's Frame Creation Model as a SoMADS.

The first five steps have two, three, one, two and then three design arenas in focus. The last four steps involve all four arenas, plus wider organisational considerations for Steps 8 and 9:

6. *Frames* (Section 4.4.1): Dorst's logical frame is modelled with a grafted connection. A ternary Frame connection replaces the Themes grafted connection. This HOW connection is from anyficiaries and antefacts (WHAT) to purpose (expected OUT-

COME). A second ternary connection is grafted from the HOW connection to evaluation and purpose. This assesses how likely a frame is to achieve the expected OUTCOME on the basis of how its HOW suggests a WHAT that could lead to it.

7. *Futures*: this has the same ADS as Frames, but develops solution antefacts further through co-evolution. Evaluation in this step focuses on whether frames lead to "realistic and viable solutions" (Dorst 2015). Frames that could have overly adverse consequences are weeded out to avoid future "paradoxes." This step's design moves cannot be fully indicated with an ADS, as they require addition and deletion of design arena. Such content detail must be provided by DAFs (Section 5.3) and DANs (Section 5.4).

8. *Transformation*: this initiates a programme of work, with a business plan, transformation agenda, and strategy for achieving results as outputs. The ADS for Frames and Futures has loops added for design arenas, which develop further here.

9. The ninth step is *Integration*, which more organisationally focused than previous steps. The outcome of Frame Creation is likely to be a design programme rather than a single project, with short "quick win" projects at the start of an overall programme for more long-term improvements. A rough SoMADS can result, with frames and their elements scheduled across episodes and projects based on how short or long term they are. A design programme will often have to go beyond the scope of an individual design project to develop Takeuchi and Nonaka's (1986) innovation factors: overlapping development phases, self-organizing project teams, built-in instability, subtle control, multilearning, and organizational transfer of learning. The latter items in this list require more organisational change than new design processes.

Modelling the FCM is a good test for SoMADS, which can fully model the first six steps. Futures cannot be fully modelled by a MADS as it requires something more concrete. Organisational aspects of transformation and Integration are beyond the scope of simply connecting design arenas.

FCM fully exploits concurrent design arenas (1–4 at once) and different connections between them (unary, binary, and ternary, concourses, simple and grafted). The potential complexity of design work is laid bare in an example of Umemoto et al.'s (2004) "frontloading," where "all project members participate [in] the earlier phases of the development process and find as many problems as possible." Even at this early point, there is anything but a clean progression, with many routes turning out to be dead ends, as Gedenryd (1998) observed for all design work. Also, as noted earlier, Koestler's (1964) *bisociation* severely underestimates what creative design work associates in parallel. Only two of seven relevant MADS are bisociative (Steps 1 and 4).

The five MADS in Figure 5.2 contrast starkly with the eight in Figure 5.3. The most complex MADS for an Engineering Design phase comes last, with three design arenas and just three binary directed connections. This linear process only *adds* design arenas and connections. In FCM, arenas enter and exit in a nonlinear manner, as do a rich range of connections. The contrast is all the greater because the nine FCM steps can be taken in a two-hour workshop, after extensive prior dialogue, whereas Engineering Design processes take weeks or months.

Design arenas are a more fundamental and more general concept than the development phases of RILED methodologies. As components of MADS they support modelling and comparison of a wide range of design processes and progressions across different design paradigms.

## 5.2   TRACKING DESIGN WORK WITH PADS

Design arenas in MADS diagrams are all the same size. In a Proportional Abstract Design Situation (PADS) diagram, sizes differ to expose balance in design work. While PADS could retain the connections of a MADS, these can distract when looking at balance of efforts and outcomes. George (2016) used PADS with three sizes for design arenas (low, medium, high). PADS were drawn both before and after activities to compare expectations with outcomes (Figure 5.4). These graphically display a reality of creative work: little can be fully planned and every activity within a design episode can bring surprises (both pleasant and unpleasant).

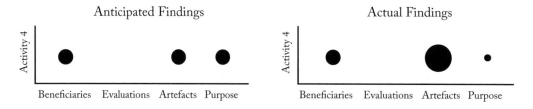

Figure 5.4: Tracking an activity using PADS (George, 2016).

PADS for particular episodes can be annotated to show, for example:

- themes in play, as in annotated portfolios (Gaver and Bowers, 2012);

- methods developed in use, e.g., using method cards (IDEO, 2003); and

- co-products such as personas, scenarios, or different forms of sketch and prototype.

Annotated PADS show at a glance dynamics of design work. PADS can share an evolving progression with stakeholders. They are also a tool for organisational learning, e.g., showing how different co-products such as sketches and prototypes in different episodes support progress of design work (Do, 1996). However, there is a limit to what can be shown in detail given the abstract level of ADS. Detail needs to be expressed separately using DAFs (overview, Section 5.3) and Notes (specifics, Section 5.4) to adumbrate content.

## 5.3     TRACKING WITH DESIGN ARENA FRAMES (DAFS)

Dorst (2015) uses three senses of "frame": two pragmatic and one logic based. His simpler pragmatic sense is an organising principle, perhaps using metaphor or analogy. A frame can capture a design arena's coherence, which an ADS cannot express. Textual representation is needed. To align with this usage, Design Arena Overviews (George, 2016) are renamed Design Arena Frames (DAFs).

Table 5.1 contains four pairs of DAFs that show design arena framing shifts at the end of the first RtD episode for George's *MyCareCircle* (see Cockton, 2020b, Chapter 6). This first episode began the shift away from a decision support system as the target artefact. The need for social networking capabilities was recognised at this point. Later shifts in framing added a library of information resources.

| Table 5.1: Reframing between episodes revealed by DAFs (George, 2016) | | |
|---|---|---|
| | **From** | **To** |
| **Artefact** | Choice and use model for decision support (DSS) tool | An embryonic comprehensive platform for multiple benefits including features for social networking. |
| **Beneficiaries** | Immediate family and child | Care circle and additional stakeholders, and child |
| **Evaluation** | No evaluation in mind | Feasibility of potential DSS was considered and discarded |
| **Purpose** | Support selection and use of Assistive Technology for a child | Support multiple benefits; plus adverse outcomes to avoid and costs to reduce |

## 5.4     TRACKING WITH DESIGN ARENA NOTES (DANS)

Dorst's second pragmatic sense for a frame is a coherent set of statements that characterise a current understanding. George (2016) developed Design Arena Progress Lists (DAPLs), which match this sense of frame, except that disparate items can be included that may indicate some lack of coherence. To indicate that this most concrete level of tracking should be an open form of verbal sketch (Eckert et al., 2012), DAPLs are renamed as Design Arena Notes (DANs), which aggregate each design arena's elements currently under consideration at varying levels of confidence and progress. They can seed or update agile backlogs and Kanbans (Cockton, 2016b).

Figure 5.5 shows combined notes for three design arenas. Each note is a simple bullet point. There are implicit concourses within Figure 5.5, specifically *implications for design* (concourse for beneficiaries and artefacts) and *implications for purpose* (concourse for beneficiaries and purpose). Co-evolution of design arenas makes Dourish's (2006) implications for design less fraught. Simply placing DANs side by side can expose tacit emerging connections between design arenas.

DANs allow incoherence and incompleteness, which has productive tensions for design. Progress is not assumed, but can become apparent when major changes to a DAN require reframing for a new DAF to capture. Significant changes to DAFs mark the end of a design episode. Goel (1995) contrasted *lateral* and *vertical* transformations in design. Lateral transformations correspond to reframings, however modest. Vertical transformations correspond to incremental additions to an arena. Dorst (2015) notes how when a frame is accepted, it can fade as routine design behaviours fall into place. As design stabilises, reframing becomes rarer and episodes become longer.

- Beneficiaries:
    - B13: The design artefact should assist inexperienced, non-professional carers (such as parents).
    - B14: Should include social workers.
    - B15: It should include additional care circle members.
- Artefacts:
    - A20: Should not impose standard care circle. This must be custom built.
    - A21: It should communicate understanding of the disabled individual's capabilities, needs, care circle membership and practices, including informal assessment by legal guardians.
    - A22: Provide initial support together with facilitation of assessment for disability intervention in a familiar environment.
    - A23: It should provide information on methods of communication to the care circle.
    - A24: It should provide information on a wide range of assessment agencies, as well as on devices and assessment and funding procedures.
- Purpose:
    - P6: It should make visits of professionals (e.g., social workers) more effective.

Figure 5.5: DAN tracking of progression (George, 2016).

DANs can have subarena groups, e.g., notes can be grouped by: stakeholders for anyficiaries; architectural levels (Garrett, 2002) for a_tefacts; and benefits, costs, and risks for purpose. Many subarena segmentations are possible. The same sets of subarenas do not need to be used for all episodes. Subarenas can change to meet the needs of specific episodes.

DANs can be structured or annotated in further ways. For example, a Kanban structure can be used to group DANs by work status, i.e., to do, in progress, complete. References to co-products link DANs to detailed design work. Other possible groupings or orderings include priority (e.g., for a MVP; Gothelf with Seiden, 2013), confidence or dependencies on incomplete work in other design arenas. Table formats can be used with columns or rows for any grouping constructs, e.g., subarenas, work status, or priority or confidence level.

One very important grouping, *interface* notes can distinguish between an internal and external focus. An interface note is (potentially) relevant to a (future) connection. This can help design teams to maintain an appropriate balance to avoid arenas becoming unconnectable silos on the one hand, versus being shallow and superficial on the other. For example, framing purpose using abstract values (e.g., human, ethical, spiritual, inner) is internally focused, begetting warm feelings but not usable interfaces for connections to other arenas. Framing design purpose as measurable specific worth (concrete benefits, costs, and risks) is externally focused, and supports connections to other arenas. Similarly, generic re-usable problem severity scales (e.g., Sauro, 2013) are internally focused within the evaluation arena, locking usability specialists in a silo by constructing severity independently of design purpose and beneficiaries.

Connections must be anticipated and prepared for. HCD's difficulties with missing interfaces is evidenced by limited *downstream utility*, the extent to evaluation results bring changes to artefacts. However, with ISO 9241-210's iteration alternatives, any phase can be immediately downstream of evaluation. Downstream utility thus involves all interfaces between evaluation and other arenas.

Poor interfaces risk turning arenas into silos, which "are the enemies of innovation" (Stevens and Moultrie, 2011). However, deficits of internally focused options risk creating shallow arenas. Creative designers must work across overlapping arenas, mediating and integrating between professional domains. However, specialists need time to develop arenas to prepare them for integration.

Explicit indication of interface notes nudges design teams to take responsibility for integratable work. RILED delegates such responsibilities to process models with very limited interfaces, although extra ones have been added. For example, the V-Model (Rook, 1986) adds interfaces beyond adjacent phases by folding a linear waterfall into a V, aligning early phases with later ones to connect back before the previous phase (Figure 5.6). Requirements specification thus provides acceptance criteria. However, there is no iterative feedback from right side testing phases to earlier left ones.

The V-model encourages us to look beyond interfaces between adjacent phases to both downstream and upstream dependencies. Poor interfaces from earlier phases to evaluations evidence *up-*

*stream futility* (Cockton, 2007b). Poor interfaces to evaluation from purpose (Cockton, 2007a) limit apt targets for evaluation measures. For example, if time on task or error counts are important, then evaluators must know how long is too long and how high is too high (Cockton, 2004a).

Design work can work back from connections or forward from design arenas. We consider these connections after considering use of ADS tracking in education and design work.

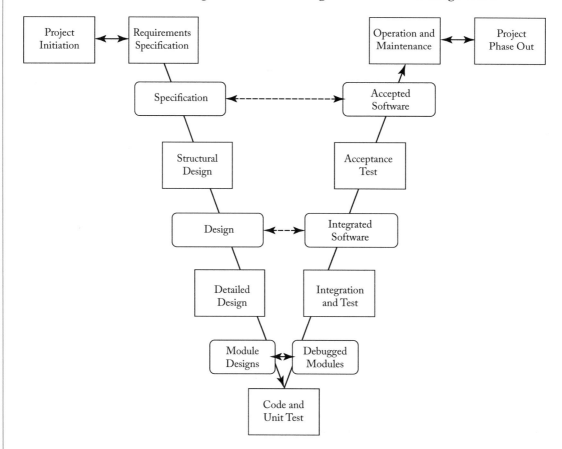

Figure 5.6: V-Model (Rook, 1986).

## 5.5   USES OF ADS CONSTRUCTS IN EDUCATION AND DESIGN WORK

ADS constructs have been used in education and professional practice. MADS and PADS have been used in teaching at all levels of Higher Education in computing and design, and in a dozen courses at international conferences, Ph.D. schools, and workshops (e.g., Cockton, 2013a). In 2016, Professional Doctorate students on the User-System Interaction (USI) programme at the Technical University of Eindhoven (TU/e) used PADS for the first week of group projects with external collaborators. Balance was tracked and adjusted on a daily basis. One reflected:

> *I was quite sceptical ... "You just drew 4 circles – and you call it a framework?" – I asked. – "No way! A framework is something that takes a lot of labour to make and a lot of effort to study! ... However, after I actually experienced some ... real work, I [can] change my mind. ... it might look simple [and] intuitive. But when you accept some of these "intuitive" things, suddenly the chaos of the creative work clears up and you see the things you actually have to do.*

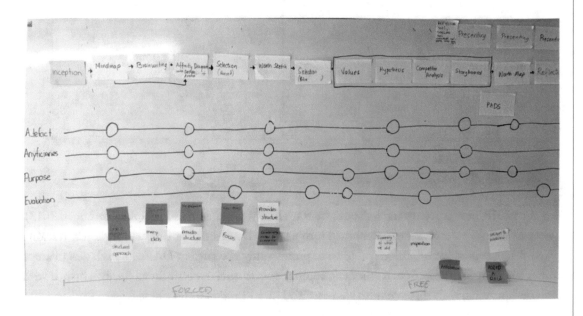

Figure 5.7: Annotated PADS by 2017 TU/e USI students, Bindu Upadhyay, Ruben Rouwhof, and Leon Neve.

Figure 5.7 shows an annotated PADS sequence on a whiteboard by a group of 2017 USI students, who worked on a week-long design sprint with a brief to improve the student experience at TU/e. Their first five activities were "forced" as part of a structured inception process. Post-its for design activities are above the PADS. (A worth analysis below the PADS uses green post-its for benefits and pink for concerns. Blue post-its record resource adaptations and extensions by the group.) All design arenas are the same size, which did not matter for the group's reflective goal.

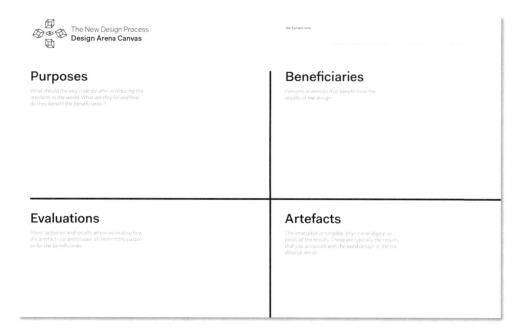

Figure 5.8: Nordkapp's design arena canvas (Korhonen, 2018).

In 2018, design arenas and episodes were trialled at Nordkapp in Helsinki (Korhonen 2018), where DANs for all arenas were combined into a single Design Arena Canvas for project tracking (Figure 5.8). A possible extension would be to prominently add current DAFs for each design arena around the central intersection. Korhonen's approach also associates traditional Kanban boards with each design arena, with three column statuses: To Do, In Progress, and Done.

## 5.6  CONNECTION NOTES (CONS)

A design situation can be thought of as a multi-arena stadium, with concourses between two or more arenas overlaid with "paths" of explicit directed connections. Notes need to be kept on connections as well as on arenas to track design work. As with DANs, Connection Notes (CoNs) are bullet points that can be grouped and annotated. DANs and CoNs begin as verbal sketches, which are later replaced either by references to co-products that evidence progress and completion, or by a later comment that deprioritises or abandons them. Chapter 4 (Cockton, 2020b) reviews a range of co-product connection resources and supporting approaches. This section considers the range of possible connections for which notes can be made.

Connections are limited and misrepresented in RILED paradigms. For example, ISO 9241-210 (ISO, 2019a) has only six unidirectional connections: three "waterfall" connections between successive phases (e.g., between understanding context of use and user requirements) and three alternative iteration connections between evaluation and the other phases (originally just one from evaluation to design). Despite this simplicity, the six connections are poorly resourced, as evidenced by difficulties with implications for design (Dourish, 2006) and upstream futility (Cockton, 2007b). Further confusion is caused by drawing arrows in the reverse direction to actual practices. Rather than following logically from a previous phase, work actually constantly refers to co-products of earlier phases. This reality of looking back is clear in both the V-Model and an argument for why rational design needs to be faked (Parnas and Clements, 1986).

In BIG design paradigms, connections between design arenas can:

- have unary, binary, ternary, or quaternary arities (Section 4.4), i,e., involve 1, 2, 3, or 4 arenas;

- be rootstock or grafted: connections can be grafted onto other connections; and

- be undirected (concourses, loops) or directed, with independent (origin) arenas and dependent (result) arenas for the latter. A binary connection has one independent (from) and one dependent (to) arena.

With four design arenas, there are four unary loops. Eleven concourses occur for other un-directed connection structures: six binary, four ternary, and one quaternary. Directed connection structures without grafts add: 12 binary connections, 24 ternary (6 connections for 3 arenas: 3 from two arenas to one and vice versa), and 14 quaternary (6 between pairs and 8 between one and the others). There are thus 65 possible connection structures before considering grafted connections (of which there are an infinite number in theory). Figure 5.9 illustrates this with each basic form of unary, binary, ternary, and quaternary connection structures, and one example graft. More complex grafted connection structures were shown in Figure 5.3. Chain and ring stuctures add further to the complexity here (Cockton, 2020b, Chapter 4). However, useful reflective analyses are possible with the simple basic forms alone.

Connections distribute focus across a_tefacts and memoranda (Section 4.4.1). The latter bring considerations to bear on an a_tefact's progress. If we think of connections as hose pipes, then the memoranda of purpose, anyficiaries and evaluations do not *centre* an a_tefact on humans, but *soak* it with so much humanity that it can absorb no further considerations about people. Design isn't a shape and it hasn't got a centre. A_tefacts repeatedly return into focus, but this need not exclude human considerations if final artefacts are *human-soaked*. The golden mean here is one of saturation. Until connections are made, a memoranda arena is not the centre of design, but a silo.

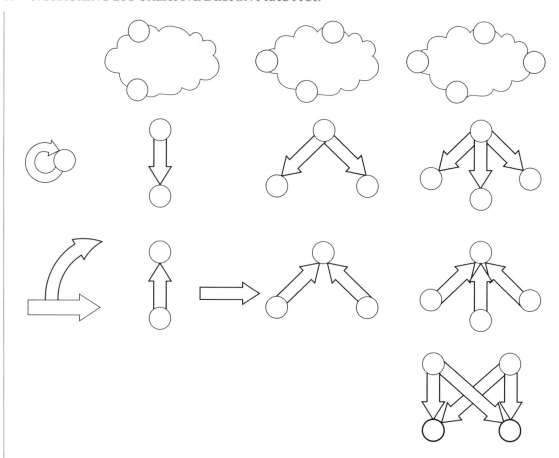

Figure 5.9: Basic and grafted connection structures in BIG Paradigms. Top row: Concourses (6 binary, 4 ternary, and 1 quaternary); 2nd row: Loop (4 in total), binary (12), ternary (12), and quaternary (4) fan outs; 3rd row: grafted connection to binary (infinite), ternary (12), and quaternary (4) fan-ins; bottom row: quaternary fan-in-fan-out (6).

Alternatives to centredness comes from concepts such as assemblies, assemblages, and actor-networks, where ideas become strategic through the connections in which they are involved. Latour (1996) writes of "careful plaiting of weak ties" and "netting, lacing, weaving, twisting of ties that are weak by themselves." This is how integration—Eames' "quality of the connections"—works. Again, we must take care with language. Along with "unfolding" (of something complete), Schön (1983) writes of "intertwining" (of co-arrivals?). The latter is ambiguous: does it mean intertwined from the outset and unravelled to reveal, or the result of adventitious work that intertwines design arenas by connecting them? The correct understanding is the latter, so we need to say *who is intertwining* and when and how, and not vaguely that design elements are intertwined. Unpicking the intertwined is eased when connections have clear interfaces to design arenas.

Saying *who is intertwining* and when and how is difficult since much design work is tacit: even in groups consensus on good connections may not need detailed elaboration (hence the concourse construct). Renn's (1992) complexities for social arenas apply to design's multi-arena stadia.

- Resource mobilization's relations to both policies and design strategy are nontrivial.

- Interacting strategies have synergistic effects that are hard to anticipate.

- Plurality of evidence and weak rules of hierarchy interact with symbolic connotations.

- Symbolic connotations connect with values and thus to contestable purpose.

- Moralization and polarization can lead to paralysis, especially when objectivity is sought.

- Design teams need pluralistic democratic contexts to reach compromise for a broad range of acceptable evidence.

- Perceptions are important; high status roles face loss of a strong position.

## 5.7   CONNECTION FRAMES (COFS)

Three different but compatible senses for a frame are (Dorst, 2015):

1. an organising principle (a pragmatic sense based on design research literature);

2. a coherent set of statements that characterise a current understanding (also pragmatic); and

3. a logical structure that relates a HOW pattern to a desirable OUTCOME.

The first is simpler than the second. The third can be seen as a formal structure for either of the others. It is (Figure 5.3, Steps 6 and 7) rooted in a ternary (2–1) connection from antefact and anyficiaries to purpose. This represents usage at a range of abstractions, providing the "patterns of relationships" for Dorst's HOW that lead from his WHAT elements (antefact and anyficiaries) to his OUTCOME (purpose). A second grafted ternary (1–2) connection assesses to what extent "observed phenomena" correspond to "desired outcomes." Beneath the superficial logic of Dorst's WHAT + HOW leads to OUTCOMES there is a complex set of relationships that first form the HOW and then evaluate the extent to which a WHAT through the HOW leads to the desired OUTCOMES.

The three senses of frame are compatible. An organising principle can be refined into a coherent set of statements, but neither require each other. Both can be refined into a logical frame to express relationships implicit in an organising principle or set of statements. However, the pragmatic senses can also apply to design arenas, with DAFs corresponding to an organising principle and DANs to a set of statements (but not necessarily a coherent set). The third logical sense can only apply to connections between arenas, which can also be expressed as an organising principle or a coherent set of statements. These verbal sketches are distinguished from DAFs as Connection Frames (CoFs). There will typically only be one DAF per design arena, but the number of CoFs has no clear limitations beyond the complexity that a design team can manage. Dorst's frames are an extreme case where only one connection frame may be required for a project, and even here, more detailed connection frames may be needed to refine the main overall framing.

Dorst's best examples of frames are organising principles, often as metaphors. For example, the Kings Cross area of Sydney was seen as a problem due to high levels of evening crime associated with drinking. Dorst's research group came up with a *music festival* framing as an organising principle that generated an innovative set of options for making changes to the Kings Cross area and associated public transport. The metaphorical framing of *like a music festival* provided a basis for a HOW that could have the desired OUTCOME of reducing crime by considering design options for a WHAT (changes to Kings Cross) that were compatible with this HOW.

1. Actual worth to
2. Assessment of
3. Achievement of
4. Target for
5. Fit with
6. Enablement of
7. Participate in
8. Preferences for
9. Reasons for
10. Focus for
11. Intended Worth for
12. Desires for

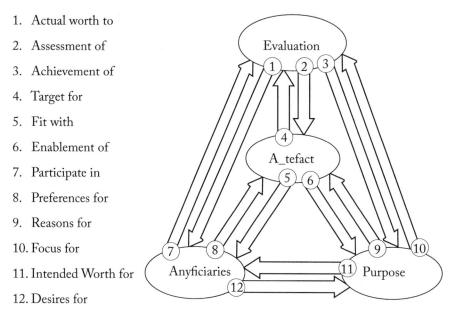

Figure 5.10: Generic framings of directed binary connections in BIG paradigms.

Dorst's frames are only one form of connection, a grafted connection that integrates all four design arenas. Other framings are possible for connections. For example, themes may group connections, e.g., Security and Safety features for cars. Here high-level abstract outcomes frame a coherent set of connections. Design teams can also be guided by generic *framings* for connections

(Figure 5.10). Framings describe the relation for a connection and are separate from its *structure* (Figure 5.9) and its *mode* (Cockton, 2020b, Section 4.1.7)

Generic framings in Figure 5.10 can be refined into specific CoFs and CoNs. For example: (1) covers practices such as participant recruitment and evaluation instructions; (6) is usage that can achieve intended purpose; and (10) develop evaluation targets for desired outcomes. Generic directed binary framings can be combined into ternary ones. For example: (6) and (12) combine into a grafted connection for *usage by a specific beneficiary*; and (7) and (10) combine into a 2:1 connection for an *evaluation plan* (Cockton, 2020b, Section 4.4.4). Connection names are inevitably compromises. For example, *Preferences for* (8) covers all indications of suitable features and capabilities, as evidenced not only be expressed preferences and requirements, but also by existing usage and experience, expertise with relevant digital technologies, and users' evaluations of existing systems.

Connections thus have structure and can be framed. They also have epistemic modes that distinguish different forms of warrant for a connection.

## 5.8 RETROSPECTIVE REPRESENTATIONS IN HCI RESEARCH THROUGH DESIGN

ADS analyses support many insights, but at a very high level of generality. More concrete tracking representations were developed by George (2016) in her Ph.D. thesis. CoNS and CoFs are a recent extension, and follow from the need to track connections in the same way as design arenas (Cockton, 2016b). This tracking operates at episode and activity level. In contrast, research through Design (RtD) practices in HCI have developed much coarser forms of overviews for use at project or programme level. These aim to communicate a creative "design process [that] seems often obliterated from descriptions of research projects" (Fallman, 2003), or misrepresented in HCI research. In addition, Wolf et al. (2006) wanted to communicate rigour in design research for a favourable comparison with dominant scientific paradigms. Their argument was based on the role of 'crits' (critiques) in studio practice in creating and maintaining consensual standards of quality.

Wolf et al. (2006) also developed one of the first substantial visualisations of creative practice in HCI for the IBM Rendezvous service, which used VoIP to let people to talk in small groups via meeting entries in their calendars. This design research project was visualised by placing images of co-products and antefacts on a timeline of swim lanes for six of Nelson and Stolterman's (2003) forms of design judgement. This showed how the project began with framing their beneficiaries and antefact, with the concept of social translucence operating as a connecting frame. This created a foundation for more detailed work on antefacts using annotated sketches to develop appearance and composition, as well as scoping Rendezvous' capabilities (further antefact framing), working tactically within the project's political constraints. As with ADS episode tracking, this visualisation facilitated shared understanding across a multidisciplinary design team. It showed how the team had been able to fulfil their initial intention, but only in hindsight: "it would have been impossible to predict or expedite our current solution."

Gaver's (2011) design workbooks can be used relatively early within a project to communicate within and beyond the design team, but have also been used in later stages with participants and collaborators. Workbooks illustrate design proposals and co-products, in a manner similar to a collection of prototypes. They are similar to the sketch or process books that are ubiquitous in educational and professional studio practice, but with a more visually finished form that can be shared beyond the design team. They use double spreads, as in magazines, and are presented to stakeholders. They are produced after initial work has slowly developed provisional ideas, explored topics, and approaches, and found important issues and perspectives.

Gaver and Bowers' (2012) annotated portfolios have a similar role to Wolf et al.'s visualisation, with annotations of designs making "clear and accountable contributions to research." Most of the example annotations can be seen as examples of Dorst's themes (Section 2.1.4), which are memoranda that can be borne in mind for future similar designs. However, the ways in which a portfolio can be annotated is open, to communicate a programme of work through multiple designs.

Representations can thus be used to track design work and to present design research during and after a project or programme. The examples above are all from RtD and may not scale to large routine projects. A simpler approach is to use a widely available design tool such as *Invision* to share design work (Convertino and Frishberg, 2020). Memoranda can be shared via comments and notes.

Wolf et al.'s timeline visualisation, design workbooks, annotated portfolios, and tools such as Invision can all complement the ADS-based representations in the previous sections. The main requirement, given that it is "impossible to predict or expedite" solutions, is that design teams have shareable representations at different abstraction levels to track progress and support reflection, deliberation, and appropriate forward planning for progressing a project.

## 5.9    CRITICAL REFLECTION AND DISCIPLINARY VALUES IN BIG DESIGN

A man sits on rocks looking out to sea. From the cliff behind him he hears shouting. He looks to confirm that the incoming tide has stranded him. He cannot swim. He looks at the cliff and sees a ledge above a tide mark. He realises that he can climb above the high tide mark to save himself.

This example is used to illustrate logical thinking in the first two pages of Stebbing's *A Modern Introduction to Logic* (1930). Beaney (2017) identifies six features of the purposive thinking here:

1. apprehension of relevant empirical facts;

2. knowledge of relevant laws or generalisation;

3. knowledge of facts about self;

4. understanding of the problem;

5. ability to reason by drawing conclusions from premises; and

6. use and understand language.

The third and sixth features are modern perspectives, but neither play a significant role in this example. Older approaches to logical reasoning would have seen the other four as adequate for practical reasoning (1 can subsume 3). They can be sequenced to form a procedure close to a RILED process: 4, 2, 1, 5. Given an understanding of the problem and knowledge of relevant laws or generalisation, once relevant empirical facts are apprehended, reason can be applied to draw conclusions. However, in creative design, these features do not arrive in the right order, and drawing conclusions can question the preceding steps (problem, laws, facts). Language can present problems and self-knowledge may not be conscious or explicit. A plan is not formed and then followed. Instead, design arenas co-evolve, as do all Beaney's features above.

George's Ph.D. (2016) and use of ADS constructs in education and professional practice have demonstrated how they support reflection *on* action (Schön, 1992) and also reflection *for* action (Killion and Todnem, 1991), where they guide the next episode of design work, along with DAFs and CoFs. They are used for reflection *on* action as part of the project tracking at the end of a design activity or episode. Reflection *for* action is particularly important for dynamic creative progressions, where design and development activities are chosen from a palette (Friedland, 2019) or programmed within a playbook (Gajander, 2019), unlike conservative processes with methods mandated for each phase. Thus, at appropriate points in creative design work, critical reflection can "fake" a rational RILED process by concluding on an episode's: current "solution" a_tefact; framing of purpose; and agreement on relevant laws and facts (memoranda). Post-hoc reasoning directs future episodes of design work.

Design work is rationalised through sensemaking, which is less concerned with truth and accuracy (both still matter) than with cue extraction, plausibility, coherence, and reasonableness. Sensemaking produces accounts that are socially acceptable and credible (Weick, 1995).

> *It would be nice if these accounts were also accurate. But in an equivocal, postmodern world, infused with the politics of interpretation and conflicting interests and inhabited by people with multiple shifting identities, an obsession with accuracy seems fruitless, and not of much practical help, either.*

The rigour of design synthesis is not the rigour of science. The aim is to develop an axiofact (Section 4.4.1) and not simply truths about the world. The worth of an axiofact must be demonstrable, a crucial task for evaluation. What happens in other design arenas and connections does not solely concern demonstrations of truth and accuracy. Much design reasoning mirrors accounts of sensemaking: retrospective, social, ongoing, involving identity, and enacted in dialogue.

Support for sensemaking from ADS constructs have been demonstrated in education, research, and practices. ADS constructs are well suited to BIG design paradigms led by creative practices, which are not RILED but CREAM (Cockton, 2017). *Aesthetic* (the "A" in CREAM) here is not to be understood as only visual, but as Aristotle's *aesthesis* (Cockton, 2018) re-expressed broadly by Heidegger as "circumspective looking" (McNeill, 1999). Aesthesis as circumspective looking is a holistic design practice that steps back from cumulative design work to reflect on progress, issues, and further work. Tracking representations support such circumspective looking.

Combining RILED with CREAM practices makes room for the engineering and management values identified in Chapter 3, but within a flexible progression that is largely creatively led, where:

- experience and intuition complement intelligence and evidence;

- discovery and subjectivity add to public knowledge;

- flexibility can be embraced without irretrievable loss of rigour;

- framing can take precedence over goals until there is confidence in design purpose;

- risk can be embraced while there are few guarantees of reliability;

- connections emerge when there is no basis for systematic translations;

- originality, openness, surprises, and ideation can be welcomed when there are no options for replication, completeness, prediction, or generation; and

- planning can be specialised for design arenas, following: human science research practices for anyficiaries and evaluation; business or other axiological ones for purpose; and creative and technical ones for a_tefacts. This avoids a single disciplinary Kanban or similar (Cockton, 2016b), and can create a "pre-backlog" of options to consider and questions to answer.

In short, when control is relaxed to allow creative freedom, there need be no tsunami of chaos. Design work will coalesce and cohere into generous solutions that cannot be planned in advance and micromanaged through PERT and Gannt charts, requirements, milestones, and deliverables.

As design activities and episodes end, creative freedom gives way to critical reflection when teams must convince themselves and clients that purpose can be achieved, subjecting designs to "rigorous testing against various constraints" including considering alternative options (Darke, 1979).

Creative work cannot be completely planned in advance, but the current state of design work can be checked over and steps taken to beneficially rationalise cumulative work. Such rationalisation is inevitably post-hoc, as it is in the creative progression of forming a mathematics proof, with moves made with a good degree of subjective intuition and experience, resulting in discoveries. Davies and Talbot (1987) share one RDI's understanding of this mix of critical rationalisation and creative ideation:

> *You do rationalise every step of the way. But I think the actual way you got them [ideas] might even be called irrational.*

If mathematical work can unapologetically move creatively first and then apply rigour, then so can creative design, where "discrete steps in a logical sequence can be infused with intuitive truth" (Davies and Talbot, 1987). As already stated (Section 3.1.5), once THE idea has been found, "fine tuning" is needed to "make it a runner" (Davies and Talbot, 1987). Outcomes matter more than process. Everything must come good through Eames' connections, Dorst's frames, or an imago.

As long as everything comes good, it doesn't have to go well at first. Tracking can expose design progression and direct design teams on their next actions across and within the arenas where detailed design work happens. However, critical reflection and deliberation requires conceptual and theoretical resources that bring depth. Tracking can provide some of this, but more is needed. Reflection and deliberation must draw on critical resources to expose gaps and concerns, and to indicate ways to address them. Book 2 (Cockton, 2020b) presents a palette of approaches and resources for worth-focused design activities and their integration with other design arenas.

## 5.10   CHAPTER SUMMARY

If we discard RILED processes and replace them with nothing, we have no basis for managing the progression of design work. We need to replace fixed processes with something. The replacement developed above is a concurrent design paradigm that is balanced and integrated, and also provides a framework for worth focused generous design.

CHAPTER 6

# CHAPTER 6

# Enabling Creative Critical Design Practices

This book has considered design work that progressively departs from a normative process as design problems get less tame. Differences between ideals and realities are primarily ones of structure. RILED phases each focus on a single design arena. Problem phases must logically precede solution phases. Systematic interfaces between adjacent phases are imagined, with phase outputs acting as inputs to generation, derivation, translation, or other design activities that are conceived as quasi-mechanical operations. None of these RILED assumptions hold in creative critical design practice.

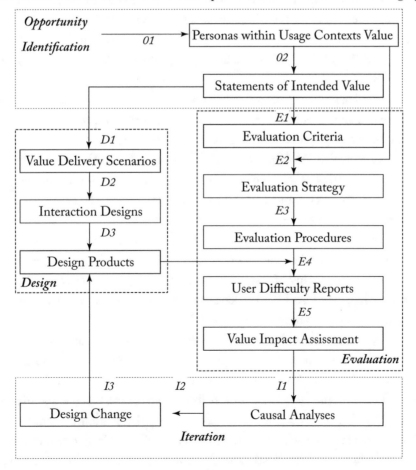

Figure 6.1: A development framework for value-centred design (Cockton, 2005).

Heskett (2005) and other design researchers write of *means* and *ends*. This book is a means to an end. This end, this book's purpose, originates in dissatisfaction with HCD and a value-centred design (VCD) response focusing IxD on value as well as quality in use and fit to context (Cockton, 2004a, 2004b). A VCD development framework (Figure 6.1) moved away somewhat from a RILED one by having four processes (dashed rectangles) rather than phases. This allows the evaluation subprocess to be interrupted by the design process. The other three processes can operate as phases as in a RILED process, but there is a basis for overlapping development phases here (Takeuchi and Nonaka, 1986).

Focusing on the RILED attributes of the VCD framework, it could be seen as iterative phase cycle starting with opportunity identification, then evaluation extending before and after design, followed by iteration. Only one process may be active at once. The internal structure of evaluation (E2, E3, E4, E5) is a RILED one, even though it starts before the design phase and pauses when that starts. It forms a strategy (E2), designs evaluation procedures (E3), implements these procedures (E4), and examines the results for their impact on achieved value (E5). The iteration phase moves from evaluation via causal analysis (I1) and design change recommendations (I2). Similarly, the structure of design (D1, D2, D3,) is a RILED one, beginning with scenarios (D1) before design (D2) and implementation (D3).

There are several departures from a RILED process structure. Evaluation starts before design, but pauses once evaluation procedures are in place. The boxes and arrows of ISO 9241-210 are swapped, placing boundary resources in boxes (e.g., Personas within Usage Contexts) and dynamic activities on arrows (e.g., E1). All but one resource is a product and the rest are co-products. All arrows indicate named activities, some of which involve 2:1 connection structures (E2 and E4). There is also a 1:2 structure (E1 and D1). Value operationalisation (E1) corresponds to framing (10: Focus for) in Figure 5.10. Processes have internal structures with co-products from one activity feeding into the next. Iteration combines analysis of evaluation results with reflection *for* action.

Departures from RILED largely follow from a critique of HCD (Cockton, 2004a, 2004b) rather than from an understanding of research into design. Purpose is derived (O2) solely from an analysis of personas in context, an HCD practice that limits the scope for of generosity. Similarly, the personas result from studies of usage contexts (O1).

There is very limited co-evolution, with evaluation pausing at the end of planning until design completes. The only "backtalk" is the single iteration connection back to design, as in the ISO13407 standard. All except two connections are one direction and binary. The two ternary connections both follow from planning evaluation before design starts. Contextual information feeds forward into both design scenarios and evaluation strategy. Evaluation procedures are ready for the finished design artefact for each iteration. However, with no understanding of ADS (Cockton, 2010a), the creation of value delivery scenarios is shown as a binary connection when it is quaternary (Cockton, 2020b, Section 4.5). However, D1's textual description has both antefacts and purpose as inputs (Cockton, 2005).

The innovations of the VCD framework were not understood and motivated by research on design work, and thus did not escape RILED constraints, as had also happened with wicked problems. As with other RILED processes, it was normative without foundations in robust design research. Over a decade has elapsed since the VCD framework was abandoned, with a new framework based on ADS constructs acting as a template (Figure 4.5) for creating BIG progressions. However, Design Thinking approaches after the VCD framework have also failed to escape RILED constraints, despite their espousal of creative design values. For example, in Google Ventures Sprint (Knapp et al., 2016), days phase design arenas: Monday for Beneficiaries; Tuesday to Thursday for Antefacts; and Friday for Evaluations. Purpose is fixed as the "Challenge" during prior planning. Creative work on antefacts refers back to previous days' implications. Arrows drawn rationally forward misrepresent actual work that checks back to connect with previous work.

We close this book by returning to questions from Chapters 1 and 3, and the Manifesto from Chapter 3. The "end" of this book is to provide foundations to remove RILED constraints on working with design purpose as value, values and worth. This creates a context where a worth-focus can be used effectively, as described in the second book. Chapter 2 presented the initial foundations, which are developed further in Chapters 4 and 5. Chapter 3 focused on RILED constraints, with the implicit analyses within the design practice research fiction fed into Chapters 4 and 5. The foundations have been developed through asking six questions.

1. What are the main areas of design work?

2. Are there standard process structures that can organise design work without regimenting it into a sequence of phases?

3. What forms and levels of abstraction would a comprehensive model of design work have?

4. What sort of connections and interfaces would be in this model?

5. What forms of tracking would a new model support?

6. What would progress look like when design work is tracked with support from a new model?

Updated answers to the first three questions, cross-referenced to Chapter 3's seven positions manifesto (e.g., M1: work areas for balanced design address, etc.) are as follows.

1. Confidence in M1, with three design arenas renamed in Chapter 4, has been maintained. The four design arenas have provided conceptual support for further original

research insights in this chapter, and have also proved to be useful in education and practice. The need for a separate purpose arena is reinforced. Without it, purpose is subordinated within another arena (as artefact specification, user needs and wants, or designers' reflective moves), and is overly constrained as a result, obstructing generosity in design and also its evaluation. Even in HCI, Carroll (1990) stressed that new technologies bring new opportunities and needs that a wholly user-centred approach would overlook.

2. The correct structure remains a highly abstract post-paradigmatic template from which specialised BIG progressions can be derived, but only post-hoc due to unavoidable adventitious elements. There is no standard process structure, but specific ones can be defined as SoMADS (Section 5.1.2), which can fall anywhere between a BIG and a RILED process. George's (2016) PADS tracking and SoMADs modelling of Dorst's (2015) FCM show how much concurrency is handled simultaneously. This supports M2: *concurrent working is the norm across areas of design work. Sequence is the exception.* M5 is also supported (*design process models should be complete at every level of their abstractions*), as there are no apparent issues with completeness for SoMADS with infinite connection potential. However, some progession dynamics cannot be made salient without adding further layers of detail with annotated PADS, DAFs, DANs, CoNs and CoFs.

3. ADS can be modelled at their most abstract by MADS and more concretely as PADS, which can be annotated to add more detail. Design arenas and connections can be framed as organising principles, or with more detail as a (coherent) set of statements. Dorst's HOW leads to OUTCOME structure is one of many framings for connections. Notes provide concrete outlines of design arenas and connections. M5 is thus further supported.

Answers to the last three questions are now possible, again cross-referenced to manifesto positions.

4. Section 5.6 has shown the range of connections. Cockton (2020b, Chapter 4) will explore the extent to which any can be preformed, but there is already evidence that M3 is too hardline (connections between work areas are created, not preformed), since Dorst's (2015) FCM can be seen as a sequence of preformed connections. Section 5.4 has developed some initial positions on interfaces between design arenas (M4: *interfaces between work areas can be prepared to support connection work*).

5. Forms of tracking include MADS, SoMADS, PADS (with annotations), DAFs, DANs, CoNs, and CoFs. Existing summarising formats from HCI research can also be used (Section 5.8). M6 is thus resourced (*design work should be tracked across work areas in ways to reveal progress*).

6. SoMADs can give an indication of progress, annotated PADS can add detail to this, and DAFs, DANs, CoNs, and CoFs can show the dynamics of design work. The extent to which the dynamics for an episode and its predecessors *indicate progress* (M6) is a matter for reflective and deliberative judgement at the ends of episodes or the activities within them. Evaluating progress is a sensemaking activity.

The six questions have all been addressed, but with only initial answers for Questions 4 and 6. The other four questions have been answered satisfactorily: there are now no clear gaps.

Language really does matter. While STEM disciplines try to tame language with technical writing style guides, the humanities embrace the wild powerful expressiveness of language. Restrictions on language in the name of objective value-free communication result in unavoidable lacunae that hide bias and oversights (Derrida, 1976/1967). It is important to have a new lexicon for design work that is free of bias, constraints, and gaps. A glossary is used in both books to gather this new lexicon in one place.

ADS analysis and synthesis provide a theoretical perspective across all extents of design work from paradigms to basic design moves. They ease effective comparison across all extents of design and provide a basis for managing concrete design situations, providing a single framework for a comprehensive range of design practices. They provide less value in the form of detailed answers to Questions 4 and 6 on connections, interfaces and progress, which will be in focus in Book 2 (Cockton, 2020b).

BIG design paradigms are virtuous in the sense that the avoid the extreme vices of RILED processes. At one extreme, HCD assumes that its siloed process can be planned alongside existing design practices without actually finding out what they are. At the other extreme, Engineering Design methodologies impose processes that ignore how design work actually operates. Indeed, a rational idealised process is seen to be useful, despite the realities of co-evolution, but is not defended on the grounds of design quality, but based on unproven assumptions about standard processes, such as follows (Parnas and Clements, 1986).

1. Designers need guidance to avoid being overwhelmed.

2. Following an unrealistic process will bring us closer to rational design.

3. It seems reasonable that a standard process, which makes "good design reviews" easier, should be rational.

4. Actual progress can be measured against an ideal process.

5. Standard processes ease the task of external review.

What is consistently striking about the above is the lack of awareness of the realities of CREAM.

1. Studio-based designers do not routinely use a standard process to handle complexity.

2. There is no value in unrealistic processes that do not value design quality.

3. Studio-based design reviews (crits) are routine and largely unproblematic.

4. Actual progress is measured against actual work and current purpose.

5. Studio-based presentations beyond the design team are routine and largely unproblematic.

BIG design paradigms flex between RILED's two vices by giving varying precedence to empirically grounded pragmatic CREAM practices over conservative RILED norms. In BIG design,
projects are:

- a sequence of multi-arena episodes (added one arena at a time in phases where apt);

- assessed through reflection on action, not compliance with plans;

- opportunistically directed through reflection for action, not rigidly pre-planned;

- flexibly open to experience, intuition, discovery, subjectivity, risk, and qualitative framing, while still able to connect intelligently with evidence and knowledge, and manage
  risk through objective quantitative targets once credible ones exist; and

- absolutely unique (Lawson, 1980).

The above can be achieved through Takeuchi and Nonaka's (1986) six success factors.

- (1) *Self-organising teams* directed through (2) *subtle management control*, rather than
  being ordered to follow unrealistic plans based on unimaginative ungenerous goals.

- Comfortable with the (3) *built-in instability* that results from (4) *overlapping development phases*.

- (5) *Organizational transfer of learning* enabled through the (6) *multi-learning* of multidisciplinary team members.

Tracking and planning overlapping development phases (4), using shared MADS, PADS,
DAFs, and DANs to manage instability (3), let teams largely self-organise (1) using multidisciplinary
expertise (6), but allow for subtle management control (2) and an audit trail for organisational transfer
of learning (5). ADS and design arena representations are deliberately simple graphically and textually,
while open to the complexity of connections across arenas and their interconnections.

BIG design drops RILED practices when they are counterproductive, but does not fill the resulting gaps with chaos. ADS and design arena representations provide tools for critical reflection and
planning. Book 2 (Cockton, 2020b) covers support for detailed work within and across design arenas.

# Glossary and Abbreviations

**A priori:** (Latin) a philosophical term for a deductive approach that proceeds from generalisations to generalisations. The derivation of Meta-Principles for Designing was a priori and considered all design arenas (Cockton, 2009).

**A_tefact:** an antefact or artefact; one of four design arenas (Cockton, 2017). Created and persistent.

**Abstract Design Situation:** a set of connected design arenas (Cockton, 2009a).

**Activation of resource function:** a design move that mobilizes a potential function of a resource.

**ADS:** Abstract Design Situation.

**ADS template:** a template that can be modified to create MADS for different design paradigms, especially BIG paradigms. Modifcation is mostly focused on connections and progressions (represented as SoMADS).

**Adventitious:** resulting from external factors or chance. Creative studio-based practices are very open to adventitious direction from insights, discoveries, accidents, fresh perspectives, etc.

**Affiliative:** a resource becomes affiliative when it improves the bonds within design teams. Activation of affiliative functions is often triggered by other functions (e.g., deliberative, integrative, invigorative). Affiliative functions were identified after Cockton (2013a).

**Agile:** a family of software design methodologies, represented in the Agile Manifesto (Beck et al., 2001), which rejects "big up front" analysis and fixed requirements to varying degrees, but always working in shorter iterative RILED cycles. There is some concurrency in agile development, but its extent beyond the artefact arena (e.g., concurrent development and testing) is contested. Concurrency in BIG applies to all design arenas, not just one.

**Ameliorative:** a resource becomes ameliorative when it activates a function that identifies positives and negatives that can contribute to an appropriate balance of worth for both the progression of design and its outcomes (axiofacts) Amelioration improves something. *Melior* is Latin for better (Cockton, 2013a).

**Antefact:** a mediating representation of a final artefact. A sketch or prototype of any form: Wizard of Oz, Paper, Lo-Fi, Hi-Fi, video, enacted (Cockton, 2017).

**Anyficiaries:** one of four design arenas. An anyficiary is a beneficiary or maleficiary. One person can be both due to a mix of benefits and sacrifices for an artefact (Cockton, 2017). A curated persistent arena.

**Approach**: coherent support for a practice, based on a set of resources. Use of an approach in design work results in a complete method once all missing resources have been added, incomplete resources completed, and other resources adapted as necessary. Approaches are rarely complete, and require additional resources to be sourced or created during design work (Woolrych et al., 2011).

**Arena**: an enclosed physical space, originally for competitive sport, combat, attention, argument, or discussion. It takes its name from its covering of *harena* (Latin, fine sand) that was laid down to absorb blood!

**Arity**: a mathematical concept that counts parameters for functions. Parameter values for a function comprise its domain. The results of applying a function to its parameters are its range. Arity is extended in this book to count all arenas in a connection, both those in the domain (origins of the connection) and its range (destinations of its connection). Most connecting transitions between RILED process phases are binary. Connections with the same arity can have different structures.

**Artefact**: the final product of design and development work, which is functional and complete. It is not a prototype (that is an antefact).

**Axiofact**: an a_tefact that demonstrably delivers worth. In research through design, this could be an antefact. In most other design situations, it must be an artefact. BIG Design creates axiofacts, not just artefacts.

**Balance**: an appropriate mix, not an equal share, of effort and outcomes across design arenas and connections. In BIG Design as a result of rejecting the big upfront planning of RILED processes.

**Beneficiary**: someone who benefits from an artefact (Cockton, 2017).

**BIG Design**: design work that is Balanced, Integrated, and Generous (Cockton, 2013b), resulting in an axiofact.

**Binary connection**: a connection of any structure between two design arenas.

**Chain of connections**: a composite connection where one connection ends at a design arena from which another connection originates. Connections within chains tend to be binary. The chain of connections is ternary or quaternary.

**Co-product**: a resource produced during design work, in contrast to an a_tefact produced by design work (Carroll, 2000). Example co-products include personas and scenarios.

**CoF**: Connection Frame.

**CoN**: Connection Notes.

**Concourse**: an open space between design arenas, a connection structure where both connections and design arenas can be implicit or latent. No DANs or DAFs need to exist. Concourses are common in the initial progression of creative design work as codes, partis, patterns, and primary generators. Design Workbooks (Gaver, 2011) and Annotated Portfolios (Gaver and Bowers, 2012) are also concourse structures.

**Concrete Design Situation**: a detailed snapshot of design work. All current work activities for a project, resources in use, and progressed resources for a design project (Dorst, 2017).

**Connection Frame**: a pragmatic framing of a connection as a textual summary, which can be part of a CoN.

**Connection Notes**: a collection of notes on connections between design arena. Each note can be a phrase, sentence or short paragraph. A connection's arity, direction, structure and mode can be noted, as can its frame. Once a connection is progressed, there will be a corresponding resource that details the work on it.

**Connection Structure**: the arity and form of a connection, which can be simple or complex. Complex structures include grafts, chains, and rings.

**CREAM**: the Creative Reflective Exploratory Aesthetic Moves (Cockton, 2017) of studio-based practices. Creative exploratory work cannot be fully planned, so reflection and deliberation are important sources of rigour. Aesthesis is an important reflective practice, understood as Heidegger's "circumspective looking" (McNeill, 1999). CREAM mixes the adventitious and the deliberate, progressing designs through work within arenas and on connections (Goldschmidt, 2014).

**Created design arenas**: a_tefacts and evaluations, arenas that have limited or no existence before a project starts, and must be specifically designed to populate them with ideas and studies, using existing approaches and resources.

**Curated design arenas**: purpose and anyficiaries, arenas that are populated with judicious selections and interpretations from external human realities, using judgement as well as research approaches.

**DAC**: Design Arena Canvas.

**DAF**: Design Arena Frame.

**DAN**: Design Arena Notes.

**Design Arena**: a sociomaterial arena (ATELIER, 2011), adding material a_tefacts and co-products to a social arena in a design setting.

**Design Arena Canvas**: A single canvas representation with a quadrant for each design arena's notes (DAN), as introduced and used at Nordkapp (Korhonen, 2018).

**Design Arena Frame**: a pragmatic frame for a design arena, written as an organising principle, perhaps using metaphor or analogy, to capture an arena's coherence, which an ADS cannot express. Originally called Design Arena Overviews (George, 2016) but renamed to align with Dorst (2015).

**Design Arena Item (DAI)**: an item in a DAN.

**Design Arena Notes**: a collection of notes on items in a design arena. Each note can be a word, phrase, sentence, or short paragraph. Once an item is progressed, there will be a corresponding resource that details the work on it. Originally called a Design Arena Progress List (George, 2016) but renamed to loosen up on the list metaphor.

**Design Paradigm**: short for Design Work Paradigm, unless otherwise stated. Paradigm is derived from "showing side by side," so that patterns may be seen. Patterns can exist at any level of abstraction in design work, from the highest-level value systems (Dorst and Dijkhuis, 1995) to specific patterns of structural design failures (Petroski, 1994).

**Design Rationale**: a set of argued connections between artefacts (features and qualities) and other design arenas (memoranda), often represented using the QOC notation.

**Design Work Paradigm**: a distinct generic pattern of working in design, expressed as a MADS. The three major design paradigms are the Applied Arts, Engineering Design, and Human-Centred Design (Cockton, 2013b).

**Domain**: in mathematics, a function's parameters. For a connection, its originating design arenas or start point(s).

**Ephemeral design arenas**: purpose and evaluations, arenas that have no existence after a project ends. Intended purpose gives way to user appropriation and evaluation results quickly lose relevance.

**Episode**: a period of multifocal design work that starts with a set of DAFs and CoFs and ends with a pause for reflection and deliberation. Episodes replace the single arena phases and stages of RILED processes. They can be time boxed like agile iterations, but they are not iterations. They are progressions (as is the project as a whole) where concurrent work in design arenas has no imposed sequences, such as Scrum's closed window rule (Cockton, 2016a).

**Evaluation**: one of four design arenas. Ephemeral and curated. With the anyficiaries arena, this includes HCD practices in BIG.

**Expressive**: a resource becomes expressive when it manifests itself in design work. Activation and realisation of expressive functions is automatic for explcit design resources (Cockton, 2013b).

**FCM**: Frame Creation Model.

**Field**: in a non-homogeneous social-spatial "field," people manoeuvre and struggle in pursuit of desirable resources (Bourdieu, 1984). Forming a field is the fifth FCM step. Synonymous with social arena.

**Frame**: An organising device or structure. Dorst (2015) has two forms of frames, logical and pragmatic (but not named or distinguished as such), which are formed in the sixth FCM step. His pragmatic form is used in DAFs and CoFs.

**Frame Creation Model**: a procedure for innovating with design frames (Dorst, 2015), beginning with intensive dialogue and research (archaeology), and proceeding through eight further stages: establishing the core paradox, themes, the context, Bordieu's field, frames, futures, transformation, and integration. Each stage can be modelled as a MADS.

**Generosity**: a meta-principle for design focused on the purpose arena, overlooked in Cockton (2009a). Core to BIG Design as a result of rejecting HCD, engineering requirements specification, or design/strategic vision as the sole basis for design purpose. Donating unexpected benefits (Cockton, 2005) is the main test of generosity. A potential with eventual diminishing returns.

**Grafted connection**: a connection to/from a connection, rather than to/from a design arena.

**HCD**: Human-Centred Design.

**HCI**: Human-Computer Interaction, knowledge from research that can support UX and IxD work, as well as contributing more generally to understanding the use and impact of interactive digital technologies.

**Human-Centred Design**: one of three major design paradigms.

**Inception**: the first episode of design work after initial approval of a project (approval may have required some design work already, which should feed into the inception).

**Informative**: a resource becomes informative when it becomes relevant to design work. Activation of informative functions occurs when introducing resources into design conversations (Cockton, 2013b).

**Integration**: connecting within, across, and between design arenas, core to BIG Design as a result of rejecting the fixed transitions of RILED processes.

**Iteration**: (1) In VCD, the fourth process. (2) In RILED processes, going around the same line again, perhaps skipping stages. Replaced by end of episode planning in BIG Design.

**IxD**: Interaction Design.

**Lacunation**: the formation of cavities in biology. Looking for such gaps (lacunae in Latin) is an important critical strategy (Derrida, 1976/1967). However, advocates of RILED processes can be so blatant about gaps (Archer, 1963/4; Parnas and Clements, 1986; Dym et al.. 2014) that there is no need for close reading or deconstruction. Such wilful disconnects with the realities of social arenas clearly expose power hierarchies in design practices. MADS have no gaps, only limitations. New design arenas and connection strucures can be added, but closure will never be achieved due to infinite possibilities for connections.

**Logical Frame**: a single format for connecting concourses (Dorst, 2015). BIG needs a much wider range of connection structures and modes, but Dorst's concept was one of the first to put structure on connections.

**Loop of connections**: a chain of connections that starts and ends with the same design arena. A complex structure for reflection and deliberation. Still hypothetical.

**MADS**: Most Abstract Design Situation.

**Maleficiary**: someone who suffers from the use of an artefact (Cockton, 2017) as a primary, secondary, or tertiary user.

**Memoranda**: (Latin) things to be borne in mind, the co-product design arenas that must be connected to an a_tefact to form an axiofact (Cockton, 2017).

**Mobilisation**: deploying resources in a social arena (Renn, 1992).

**Most Abstract Design Situation**: an ADS that only indicates the presence/absence of design arenas and connections. Only an ADS template is more abstract.

**Multifocal**: having a focus on more than one design arena.

**MVP**: a Minimal Viable Product, a Lean concept (Gothelf with Seiden, 2013), is an artefact with the minimal set of capabilities for success in a market.

**Opportunity Identification**: the first VCD process (Cockton, 2005), renamed to Worth Identification by (Vu, 2013).

**Organisation**: an alternative name for Institution as understood for L-ERG-IKK, but useful as a generalisation of design's beneficiaries with the "growing recognition that the main arena in which design is practiced is not business, but the organization" (Junginger, 2017).

**PADS**: Proportional Abstract Design Situation.

**Palette**: a design team's repertoire of resources, approaches, and progression patterns (Friedland, 2019).

**Parti**: short for *parti pris* (French), a departure point, a concourse beyond the Primary Generator, a conjecture with some analysis (Stolterman, 1999). The term originates in architecture, along with charette.

**Pattern**: a more explicit concourse than codes, a semi-structured mix of design arenas with implicit and explicit connections (Alexander et al., 1977).

**Performative**: a resource becomes performative when it is used in social settings to inform, account, or persuade. Performative functions are activated by the anticipation of a social setting (Cockton, 2013a).

**Persistent design arenas**: artefact and anyficiaries, arenas that continue to exist after a project ends. Artefacts persist as long as the programmes that support them. Anyficiaries precede and outlive products and programmes.

**Playbook**: a palette with an overlay of something akin to codes (Hillier et al., 1972) that triggers specific plays of resources, approaches, and progression patterns in specific contexts for design work (Gajander, 2019).

**Pragmatic Frame**: an organising principle, perhaps using metaphor or analogy, or elaborated as a coherent set of statements that characterise a current understanding (Dorst, 2015). A more useful framing of frames than logical frames.

**Primary Generator**: an antecedent of a proposed solution or conjecture (Darke, 1979); a concourse structure spanning the antefact and other design arenas.

**Product**: the "goods or services" (Junginger, 2017) developed by or for any organisation, regardless of sector (private, public, voluntary).

**Programme**: a co-ordinated series of projects to develop and maintain a product or product line (i.e., a family of related products such as an app, website, and kiosk).

**Progression**: a narrative of design work (Jones, 2020). What actually happens in a design project, as opposed to what should happen according to some imposed normative idealised process.

**Proportional Abstract Design Situation**: an ADS that shows extents of effort and/or results for each design arena. Connections are usually omitted and design arena indicators laid out in rows (George, 2016).

**Purpose**: one of four design arenas. This ephemeral curated arena does not exist in any major design paradigm, but is absorbed into others by Applied Arts (designer's vision), Engineering Design (requirements specifications), and HCD (users' needs, wants, and pain points).

**Quaternary connection**: a connection of any structure between four design arenas.

**Resource**: any co-product, knowledge, or element of practice that can support design research. Resources are mobilized by activating and realising potential functions. Activation is rarely automatic. Resources typically require work to set them to work.

**RILED**: Rational Idealised Linear Engineering Design (Parnas and Clements, 1986), a normative process model with no basis in fact and contrary to 50 years on creative design.

**Rootstock connection**: a simple connection onto which another connection is grafted.

**Secondary user**: a stakeholder who does not use an interactive artefact but has some responsibility (e.g., as a manager supplier or parent) towards primary users who do (and may thus benefit or suffer indirectly).

**Simple Connection**: a single connection of any arity, with no grafts.

**Sociomaterial**: an assemblage of social and material (including human bodies) phenomena (ATELIER, 2011; Dourish, 2001).

**SoMADS**: a sequence of MADS, representing process, procedure, and progression using a MADS for each phase, stage, step, and episode of activity.

**Subarena**: any subdivision of a design arena. Subarenas can nest. Overlapping sets of subarenas are common. For example, the anyficiary subarena sets (beneficiaries, maleficiaries) and (primary users, secondary users, tertiary users) overlap. Suppliers are a subarena of secondary users. Sponsors could be a subarena of secondary or tertiary users depending on how the achieved worth of a system impacts them.

**Ternary connection**: a connection of any structure between three design arenas.

**Tertiary user**: a stakeholder who does not use an interactive artefact and has no responsibility for primary users who do (e.g., an associate of someone with accessibility problems, the public sphere for fake news), but who still benefit or suffer indirectly.

**UCD**: User-Centred Design.

**Unary connection**: a connection from a design arena to itself, indicating a significant change to it as a result of a current activity or episode. An additional grafted connection indicates when changes originate from another arena.

**User-Centred Design**: an extremist approach to design that only cares about primary users, ignoring other anyficiaries and related purpose.

**Value**: something beneficial that is appraised positively.

**Value-Centred Design**: a relaxed RILED framework of four processes for: positive design purpose, evaluation (planned before designing, resumed when test a_tefact beomes available), design, and iteration. Iteration is a process that plans what to do next based on whether value has been donated, delivered, degraded, destroyed, or denied (Cockton, 2005). Vu (2013) renamed the processes to align them with WCD (Cockton, 2006).

**Values**: abstract reifications that guide human behaviours and appraisals towards positives.

**VCD**: Value-Centred Design.

**WCD**: Worth-Centred Design.

**Wo-Fo**: Worth-Focused, a more balanced concept than worth-centred. Some design activities are worth-focused, others aren't. Design is a complex multifocal activity that cannot have a single centre without causing imbalance and distortion (Cockton, 2013b).

**Worth**: a sufficiently positive balance of benefits over sacrifices (costs, risks) that motivates people to buy, learn, use or recommend an interactive digital artefact (Cockton, 2006).

**Worth-Centred Design**: a revision of VCD that replaced value with worth and opportunity identification with a broader focus on individual and collective value (Cockton, 2006).

# References

Alexander, C., Ishikawa, S., and Silverstein, M. with Jacobson, M.,Fiksdahl-King, I., and Angel, S. 1977. *A Pattern Language: Towns, Buildings, Construction*. Oxford. 125

Al-Maria, S., Alleyne, A., Baines, P., Boyce, S., Carpenter, E., Carrington, N., Davies, S., Deacon, R., Deakin, F., Dunhill, M., Farthing, S., Hiorns, R., Katrantzou, M., King, S., Morton, T, Norman, N., Orta, L., Perry, G., Raban, W., Rapley, J., Rughani, P., Smith, B and R., Storey, H., tide-Frater, S., Triggs, T., deWaal, E., and Zeegen, L. 2016. *The Creative Stance*. Cornerhouse Publications. 9

Archer, L. B. 1963/4. Systematic method for designers. *Design*. 59

Ardito, C., Baldassarre, M. T., Caivano, D., and Lanzilotti, R. 2016. Integration of human-centred design and agile software development practices: Experience report from a SME. *Integrating User-Centered Design in Agile Development*, eds. Cockton, G. Lárusdóttir, M.L., Gregory, P., and Cajander, Å. 117–135, Springer. DOI: 10.1007/978-3-319-32165-3_5. 50

Arrow, K. J. and Fischer, A. C. 1974. Environmental preservation, uncertainty and irreversibility. *Quarterly Journal of Economics,* 88(2), 312–9. DOI: 0.2307/1883074. 17

ATELIER (Project: Thomas Binder, Giorgio De Michelis, Pelle Ehn, Giulio Jacucci, Per Linde, and Ina Wagner). 2011. *Design Things*. MIT Press. 61

Atman, C., Yasuhara, K., Adams, R., Barker, T., Turns, J., and Rhone, E. 2008. Breadth in problem-scoping: A comparison of freshman and senior engineering students. *International Journal of Engineering Education*, 24(2), 234–245. 14

Beaney, M. 2017. *Analytic Philosophy: A Very Short Introduction*. Oxford. DOI: 10.1093/actrade/9780198778028.001.0001. 108

Beck, U. 1992. *Risk Society: Towards a New Modernity*. Sage. xx, 79, 80

Beck, K., Beedle, M., Van Bennekum, A., Cockburn, A., Cunningham, W., Fowler, M., Grenning, J., Highsmith, J., Hunt, A., Jeffries, R., Kern, J., Marick, B., Martin, R. C., Mellor, S., Schwaber, K., Sutherland, J., and Thomas D. 2001. *Manifesto for Agile Software Development*, http://www.agilemanifesto.org. 119

Biedenbach, T. and Jacobsson, M. 2016. The open secret of values: The roles of values and axiology in project research. *Project Management Journal,* 47(3), 139–155. DOI: 10.1177/875697281604700312. xv

Blythe, M. and Encinas, E. 2016. The co-ordinates of design fiction: Extrapolation, irony, ambiguity and magic. *Proceedings of the 19th International Conference on Supporting Group Work (GROUP '16)*, ACM, 345–354. DOI: 10.1145/2957276.2957299. 31

Bourdieu, P. 1984. *Distinction: A Social Critique of the Judgement of Taste.* Routledge. 61

Bradley, C., Hirt, M., and Smit, S. 2018. *Strategy Beyond the Hockey Stick: People, Probabilities, and Big Moves to Beat the Odds.* Wiley. 66

Brown, T. 2009. *Change by Design: How Design Thinking Transforms Organizations and Inspires Innovation.* Harper Business. xvi

Bruner, J. S. 1985. Narrative and paradigmatic modes of thought. *Learning and Teaching the Ways of Knowing.* Ed., Eisner, E. W. University of Chicago Press, 97-115. 23

Buchanan, R. 1992. Wicked problems in design thinking. *Design Issues*, 8(2), 5–21. DOI: 10.2307/1511637. 11

Card, S. K., Moran, T. P., and Newell, A. 1983. *The Psychology of Human-Computer Interaction.* Lawrence Erlbaum Associates. 23

Carroll, J. M. 1990. Infinite detail and emulation in an ontologically minimized HCI. *Proceedings Conference on Human Factors in Computing Systems (CHI '90)*, eds. Chew, J. C. and Whiteside, J). ACM, 321–328. DOI: 10.1145/97243.97303. 67, 116

Carroll, J. M. 2000. *Making Use: Scenario-Based Design of Human-Computer Interactions.* Cambridge, MA: MIT Press. 23, 59, 61

Christensen, C. M. and Kaufman, S. P. 2008. Innovation killers: How financial tools destroy your capacity to do new things. *Harvard Business Review,* 86(1), 98–105. 31

Cockton, G. 1990. Designing abstractions for communication control. *Formal Methods in Human Computer Interaction*, eds. Harrison, M.D. and Thimbleby, H.W. Cambridge University Press, 233–271. 68

Cockton, G. 1993. Spaces and distances: software architecture and abstraction and their relation to adaptation. *Adaptive User Interfaces, Principles and Practice*, eds. Schneider-Hufschmidt, M., Kühme, T., and Malinowski, U. North-Holland, 79–108. 68

Cockton, G. 2004a. From quality in use to value in the world. *CHI 2004 Extended Abstracts*, ACM, 1287–90. DOI: 10.1145/985921.986045. xvii, 100, 114

Cockton, G. 2004b. Value-centred HCI. *Proceedings Third Nordic Conference on Human-Computer Interaction*, ed. Hyrskykari, A. 149–160. DOI: 10.1145/1028014.1028038. xvii, 114

Cockton, G. 2005. A development framework for value-centred design. *CHI 2005 Extended Abstracts*, ed. Gale, C. ACM, 1292–95. DOI: 10.1145/1056808.1056899. 73, 93, 113, 115

Cockton, G. 2006. Designing worth is worth designing. *Proceedings NordiCHI 2006*, eds. Mørch, A. I., Morgan, K., Bratteteig, T., Ghosh, G., and Svanæs, D. 165–174. DOI: 10.1145/1182475.1182493. xvii

Cockton, G. 2007a. Make evaluation poverty history, alt.chi paper, *CHI 2007*, available from https://www.academia.edu/1906725/Make_Evaluation_Poverty_History. DOI: 10.1145/1240624.2180964. 76, 78, 99

Cockton, G. 2007b. Upstream futility blocks downstream utility. *Downstream Utility: The Good, the Bad, and the Utterly Useless Usability Evaluation Feedback*, eds. Law, E.L-C., Lárus-dóttirM.K., and Nørgaard, M. 100–105. https://www.irit.fr/recherches/ICS/projects/cost294/upload/495.pdf. 99, 103

Cockton, G. 2008b. Revisiting usability's three key principles. *CHI 2008 Extended Abstracts*, 2473–2484. DOI: 10.1145/1358628.1358704. xix, 31

Cockton, G. 2008d. Sketch worth, catch dreams, be fruity. *CHI 2008 Extended Abstracts*, eds. Czerwinski, M., Lund, A. M., and Tan, D.S. 2579–2582. DOI: 10.1145/1358628.1358716. xix, 31

Cockton, G. 2009a. Getting there: Six meta-principles and interaction design. *Proceedings CHI 2009*, eds. Olsen Jr., D. R., Arthur, R. B., Hinckley, K., Morris, M. R., Hudson, S., and Greenberg, S. ACM, 2223–2232. xviii, 31

Cockton, G. 2010a. Design situations and methodological innovation in interaction design. *CHI 2010 Extended Abstracts*, eds. Mynatt, E. D., Schoner, D., Fitzpatrick, G., Hudson, S. E., Edwards, K. and Rodden, T. ACM, 2745–2754. DOI: 10.1145/1753846.1753859. 58, 81, 82, 90, 114

Cockton, G. 2010b. Inclusion requires inclusiveness. *Proceedings DSAI 2010*, eds. Gnanayutham, P., Paredes, H. and Rekanos, I. T. 15-22, UTAD. Available from https://researchportal.port.ac.uk/portal/files/131731/DSAI2010_Proceedings_Book.pdf. xviii, 15

Cockton, G. 2012a. UCD: Critique via parody and a sequel. *CHI 2012 Extended Abstracts*, ACM, 1–10. DOI: 10.1145/2212776.2212778. xix, 31, 51

Cockton, G. 2012b. Refuser (centered design): moving on, moving out, moving up. Blogspot. *Interactions,* 19(6), 8–9. DOI: 10.1145/2377783.2377786. xix

Cockton, G. 2013a. You (have to) design design, co design. Included *Wer gestaltet die Gestaltung? Praxis, Theorie und Geschichte des partizipatorischen Designs.*, eds, Mareis, C., Held, M., and Joost, G., Bielefeld: transcript. 181–205. xviii, 64, 100

Cockton, G. 2013b. Design isn't a shape and it hasn't got a centre: thinking BIG about post-centric interaction design. *Proceedings MIDI '13*, ACM, Article 2. DOI: 10.1145/2500342.2500344. xviii, 70

Cockton, G. 2013c. A load of cobbler's children: beyond the model designing processor. *CHI '13 Extended Abstracts on Human Factors in Computing Systems*, ACM, 2139–2148. DOI: 10.1145/2468356.2468733. xix, 31

Cockton, G. 2014. A critical, creative UX community: CLUF. *Journal of Usability Studies*, 10(1), 1–16. Invited Editorial, available at http://uxpajournal.org/a-critical-creative-ux-community-cluf/. 65

Cockton, G. 2016a. Integrating both user-ccentred design and creative practices into agile development, in *Integrating User-Centered Design in Agile Development*, eds. Cockton, G., Lárusdóttir, M. L., Gregory, P., and Cajander, Å. , Springer, 1–46. DOI: 10.1007/978-3-319-32165-3_1. 19, 49, 50

Cockton, G. 2016b. Five kanbans for better balanced agile development, Position paper for *NordiCHI 2106 Workshop on Stakeholder Involvement in Agile Software*. Available at https://stakeholdersinagile.wordpress.com/papers/. 89, 97, 107, 110

Cockton, G. 2017. New process, new vocabulary: Axiofact = A_tefact + Memoranda, *CHI '17 Extended Abstracts on Human Factors in Computing Systems (CHI EA '17)*, ACM, 747–757. DOI: 10.1145/3027063.3052755. xix, 19, 31, 54, 55, 67, 85, 91, 110

Cockton, G. 2018. Way back to a design future: Aristotle's intellectual excellences and their implications for designing. *Critical Theory and Interaction Design*, eds. Bardzell, J., Bardzell, S., and Blythe, M. MIT Press, 287–309. 53, 110

Cockton, G. 2020b. *Worth-Focused Design: Book 2: Approaches, Contexts, and Case Sstudies*. Morgan & Claypool, San Rafael, CA. DOI: 10.2200/S01000ED1V02Y202003HCI047. xxii, 18, 23, 29, 58, 70, 82, 83, 87, 97, 102, 103, 107, 111, 115, 116, 117, 118

Cockton, G. 2057. All my papers had wrong bits in them, but I have finally solved all the problems in HCI. *Journal of Perfect Answers to Everything*, 1(1), 1–2. 31

Cockton, G. and Clarke, S. 1999. Using contextual information effectively in design, *INTERACT 99 Proceedings*, eds. Sasse, A. and Johnson, C., 578–585. xvi

Cockton, G., Clarke, S., Gray, P. D., and Johnson, C. 1996. Literate development: Weaving human context into design specifications. *Critical Issues in User Interface Systems Engineering*, eds. Benyon, D. and Palanque, P. Springer Verlag, 227–248. DOI: 10.1007/978-1-4471-1001-9_13. 68

Cockton, G., Kirk, D., Sellen, A., and Banks, R. 2009a. Evolving and augmenting worth mapping for family archives. *Proceedings HCI 2009*, 329–338, BCS. DOI: 10.14236/ewic/HCI2009.40. xvii

Cockton, G., Woolrych, A., Hall, L., and Hindmarch, M. 2003. Changing analysts' tunes: The surprising impact of a new instrument for usability inspection method assessment. *People and Computers XVII: Designing for Society*, eds.Palanque, P., Johnson, P., and O'Neill, E. Springer-Verlag, 145–162. DOI: 10.1007/978-1-4471-3754-2_9. xvi

Cockton, G., Gregory, P., Lárusdóttir, M. L., and Cajander, Å. 2016. Introduction. Integrating user-centred design in agile development. *Integrating User-Centered Design in Agile Development*, eds. Cockton, G., Lárusdóttir, M. L., Gregory, P., and Cajander, Å. , Springer, 1–46. DOI: 10.1007/978-3-319-32165-3_1. 17

Conklin, J. 2005. *Dialogue Mapping: Building Shared Understanding of Wicked Problems.* Wiley. 77

Convertino, G. and Frishberg, N. 2020. Impact through alliances: two stories. *Interactions*, 27(1),77–79. DOI: 10.1145/3371289. 67, 71, 79, 108

Cross, N. 1997. Creativity in design: Analyzing and modeling the creative leap. *Leonardo*, 30(4).311–317. DOI: 10.2307/1576478. 21, 90

Cross, N. 2011. *Design Thinking: Understanding How Designers Think and Work.* Berg. DOI: 10.5040/9781474293884. 13, 14, 15, 28

Darke, J. 1979. The primary generator and the design process. *Design Studies,* 1(1), 36–44. DOI: 10.1016/0142-694X(79)90027-9. 14, 18, 22, 23, 28, 41, 43, 45, 51, 84, 90, 91, 110

Davies, R. and Talbot, R. 1987. Experiencing ideas; identity, insight and the imago. *Design Studies*, 8(1), 17–25. DOI: 10.1016/0142-694X(87)90027-5. 11, 13, 21, 22, 44, 54, 82, 85, 111

Derrida, J. 1976. *Of Grammatology* (G. Spivak's translation of De La Grammatologie 1967). Johns Hopkins University Press. 18, 117

Dilnot, C. 2017. Introduction and notes on editing the manuscript. *Design and the Creation of Value*, eds. Dilnot, C. and Boztepe, S. Bloomsbury, 1–20, 39–42. DOI: 10.5040/9781474274289.0007. xvii

Do, E. Y-L. 1996. The right tool at the right time: An investigation of freehand drawing as an interface to knowledge based design systems. *ACADIA, Proceedings of Association for Computer Aided Design in Architecture*, University of Arizona, 191–199. 96

Doblin, J. 1978. *Innovation: A Cook Book Approach*. Doblin. Available from https://doblin.com/our-thinking/innovation-a-cook-book-approach. 10, 11

Doherty, E. P. Cockton, G., Bloor, C., and Benigno, D. 2000. Mixing oil and water: Transcending method boundaries in assistive technology for traumatic brain injury. *Proceedings ACM 1st Conf. on Universal Usability*, eds. Sholtz, J. and Thomas, J. ACM, 110–117. DOI: 10.1145/355460.355544. 55

Dorst, K. 2015. *Frame Innovation: Create New Thinking by Design*. MIT Press. DOI: 10.7551/mitpress/10096.001.0001. 9, 10, 11, 12, 19, 22, 25, 28, 29, 54, 59, 61, 66, 79, 82, 83, 84, 90, 93, 95, 97, 98, 105, 116

Dorst, K. 2017. *Notes on Design: How Creative Practice Works*. BIS. 9, 31, 49, 54, 59, 60

Dorst, K. and Dijkhuis, J. 1995. Comparing paradigms for describing design activity. *Design Studies*, 16(2), 261–274. DOI: 10.1016/0142-694X(94)00012-3. 69, 70

Dourish, P. 2001. Where the Action Is: The Foundations of Embodied Interaction. MIT Press. 126

Dourish, P. 2006. Implications for design. *Proceedings of the SIGCHI Conference on Human Factors in Computing Systems (CHI '06)*, eds. Grinter, R., Rodden, T., Aoki, P., Cutrell, E., Jeffries, R., and Olson, G. ACM, 541–550. DOI: 10.1145/1124772.1124855. 46, 75, 98, 103

Dreyfuss, H. 1955. *Designing for People*. Simon & Schuster. 71

Dym, C. 1994. *Engineering Design: A Synthesis of Views*. Cambridge. 42, 54, 72

Dym, C. and Little, P. 2009. *Engineering Design: A Project Based Introduction*, 3rd ed. Wiley. 35

Dym, C. L., Little, P., and Orwin, E. J. 2014. *Engineering Design: A Project Based Introduction*, 4th ed. Wiley. 21, 38, 39, 43. 46, 52, 59, 73, 74

Eckert, C. M. and Stacey, M. K. 2010. What is a process model? Reflections on the epistemology of design process models. *Modelling and Management of Engineering Processes*, eds. Heisig, P., Clarkson, J., and Vanja, S. Springer, 3–14. DOI: 10.1007/978-1-84996-199-8_1. 14

Eckert, C., Blackwell, A., Stacey, M., Earl, C., and Church, L. 2012. Sketching across design domains: Roles and formalities. *Artificial Intelligence for Engineering Design, Analysis and Manufacturing*, 26(3), 245-266. DOI: 10.1017/S0890060412000133. 97

Erhorn, C. and Stark, J. 1995. *Competing by Design: Creating Value and Market Advantage in New Product Development*. Wiley. 41

Erickson, T. 1996. Design as storytelling. *Interactions*, 30–35 (July). DOI: 10.1145/234813.234817. 23

Fallman, D. 2003. Design-oriented human-computer interaction. In *Proceedings of the SIGCHI Conference on Human Factors in Computing Systems (CHI '03)*, ACM, 225–232. DOI: 10.1145/642611.642652. 8, 25, 26

Fanon, F. 1967. *Black Skin, White Masks* (translated by Charles Lam Markmann). Pluto. 18, 51, 59, 68, 69, 70, 71, 80, 85, 107

Field, D. 2017. 6 major tech companies have doubled their design hiring goals in last half decade. *Techcrunch*. https://techcrunch.com/2017/05/31/here-are-some-reasons-behind-techs-design-shortage/. 48

Frayling, C. 1993. *Research in Art and Design*. Royal College of Art. 1(1). xvii, 8, 26

Friedland, L. 2019. Culture eats UX strategy for breakfast. *Interactions*, 26(5), 78–81. DOI: 10.1145/3344947. xix, 5, 109

Gajendar, U. 2019. Toward a playbook for UX leaders. *Interactions*, 26(2), 24-25. DOI: 10.1145/3305354. xix, 5, 109

Garnik, I., Sikorski, M., and Cockton, G. 2014. Creative sprints: an unplanned broad agile evaluation and redesign process. *Proceedings NordiCHI '14*, ACM, 1125–1130. DOI: 10.1145/2639189.2670290. 65

Garrett, J. J. 2002. *The Elements of User Experience: User-Centered Design for the Web*. New Riders Publishing. 98

Garrett, J. J. 2002. *The Elements of User Experience: User-centered Design for the Web*. New Riders. DOI: 10.1111/j.1948-7169.2006.tb00027.x. 68

Gaver, W. 2011. Making spaces: how design workbooks work. *Proceedings SIGCHI Conference on Human Factors in Computing Systems (CHI '11)*, ACM, 1551–1560. DOI: 10.1145/1978942.1979169. 25, 28, 31, 59, 79, 85, 108

Gaver, W. and Bowers, J. 2012. Annotated portfolios. *Interactions*, 19(4), 40–49. DOI: 10.1145/2212877.2212889. 9, 10, 11, 19, 20, 22, 27, 45, 85, 96, 108

Gedenryd, H. 1998. How designers work: Making sense of authentic cognitive activities. Lund University Cognitive Studies 75. Available from https://lup.lub.lu.se/search/publication/d88efa51-c2f9-4551-a259-00bd36fe8d03. 18, 19, 22, 25, 32, 41, 53, 54, 66, 68, 74, 83, 90, 95

George, J. 2016. A case study of balance and integration in worth-focused research through design, Ph.D. thesis, Northumbria University. http://nrl.northumbria.ac.uk/30326/. xviii, xxii, 82, 89, 91, 96, 97, 98, 107, 109, 116

Goel, V. 1995. *Sketches of Thought*. MIT Press. 98

Goldschmidt, G. 2014. *Linkography: Unfolding the Design Process.* MIT Press. DOI: 10.7551/mit-press/9455.001.0001. 22, 68

Good, M., Spine, T. M., Whiteside, J., and George, P. . 1986. User-derived impact analysis as a tool for usability engineering. *Proceedings of the SIGCHI Conference on Human Factors in Computing Systems (CHI '86).* ACM 241–246. DOI: 10.1145/22627.22378. 23

Gothelf, J. with Seiden, J. 2013. *Lean UX: Applying Lean Principles to Improve User Experience.* O'Reilly. 99

Gould, J. and Lewis, C. 1985. Designing for usability: Key principles and what designers think. *CACM,* 28(3). 300–311. DOI: 10.1145/3166.3170. 23, 39, 50, 62, 65, 74, 76

Gray, W. D. and Salzman, M. C. 1998. Damaged merchandise? A review of experiments that compare usability evaluation methods. *HCI,* 13(3), 203–261. DOI: 10.1207/s15327051hci1303_2. 64

Guindon, R. 1990. Designing the design process: exploiting opportunistic thoughts. *Human-Computer Interaction,* 5(2), 305–344. DOI: 10.1207/s15327051hci0502&3_6. 14

Hartson, H. R. and Hix, D. 1989. Toward empirically derived methodologies and tools for human-computer interface Development. *International Journal of Man-Machine Studies,* 31, 477–494. DOI: 10.1016/0020-7373(89)90005-9. 76

Hegarty, J. 2014. *Hegarty on Creativity: There Are No Rules.* Thames & Hudson. 9

Heskett, J. 2005. *Design: A Very Short Introduction.* Oxford. DOI: 10.1093/actrade/9780192854469.001.0001. 4, 19, 20, 56, 60, 63, 81, 89, 90, 114

Heskett, J. 2017. *Design and the Creation of Value,* eds. Dilnot, C. and Boztepe, S. Bloomsbury. DOI: 10.5040/9781474274289. xvii, 15, 16, 41

Hillier, B., Musgrove, J., and O' Sullivan, P. 1972. Knowledge and design. *Environmental Design: Research and Practice,* edra3/ar8 conference, ed. Mitchell, W. UCLA. 9

IDEO. 2003. *IDEO Method Cards: 51 Ways to Inspire Design.* IDEO Palo Alto. 96

ISO. 2019a. Human-centred design for interactive systems. *Ergonomics of Human System Interaction Part 210 (ISO 9241–210).* International Organization for Standardization. 7, 14, 102

ISO. 2019b. *Systems and software engineering—Software product Quality Requirements and Evaluation (SQuaRE)—Common Industry Format (CIF) for Usability: User Requirements Specification.* (ISO 25065:2019). International Organization for Standardization. 64

Jeffries R., Turner A. A., Polson P. G. and Atwood, M. E. 1981. The processes involved in designing software. *Cognitive Skills and their Acquisition,* ed. Anderson J. R., Lawrence Erlbaum, 255–283. 24, 25

Jones, J. C., 1970. *Design Methods*. 1st ed. Van Nostrand Reinhold. 8, 68

Jones, J. C. 1988. Softecnica. *Design After Modernism: Beyond the Object*, ed. Thackera, J., Thames and Hudson, 216–266. 8

Jones, M. 2020. Making scenarios more worthwhile: Orienting to design story work, Ph.D. thesis, Northumbria University. http://nrl.northumbria.ac.uk/xxxx/. xxii

Joost, G., Nieters, J., and Bollman, E. 2010. *Practicing Innovation: Methods for Practicing Innovation in Your Daily Work, Design Research Lab/T-Labs*. Berlin & Yahoo Inc., New York. 23

Junginger, S. 2017. Design as an economic necessity for governments and organisations. *Design and the Creation of Value*, eds. Dilnot, C. and Boztepe, S.,30–37. Bloomsbury. DOI: 10.5040/9781474274289.0006. 12, 15, 20, 61, 62, 66

Kalbach, J. 2019. Maximize business impact with JTBD. *Interactions,* 26(1), 80-83. DOI: 10.1145/3292021. 49, 66

Karat, J. (ed). 1991. *Taking Software Design Seriously: Practical Techniques for Human/Computer Interaction*, Elsevier. 45

Killion, J. P. and Todnem, G. R. 1991. A process of personal theory building. *Educational Leadership,* 48(6), 14–17. 82, 109

Kitschelt, H. P. 1980. *Kernerenergiepolitik: Arena eines gesellschaftlichen Konflikts*. Campus Verlag. 61, 73

Knapp, J., Zeratsky, J., and Kowitz, B. 2016. *Sprint: How to Solve Big Problems and Test New Ideas in Just Five Days*. Simon & Schuster. 29, 49, 115

Koestler, A. 1964. *The Act of Creation*. Hutchinson. DOI: 10.1177/000271626536000141. 85, 95

Kolko, J. 2010. Abductive thinking and sensemaking: The drivers of design synthesis. *Design Issue,s* 26(1), 15–28. DOI: 10.1162/desi.2010.26.1.15. 63

Kolko, J. 2015. *Exposing the Magic of Design: A Practitioner's Guide to the Methods and Theory of Synthesis*. Oxford. 22, 90

Korhonen, P. 2018. Re-thinking design thinking: Part VII: The new design process in brief. https://blog.nordkapp.fi/re-thinking-design-thinking-part-vii-the-new-design-process-in-brief-aa59aa099c7. 102

Krippendorff, K. 2005. *The Semantic Turn; A New Foundation for Design*. Taylor & Francis. DOI: 10.4324/9780203299951. 13, 71

Lash, S. and Wynne, B. 1994. Introduction. Ulrich Beck, *Risk Society: Towards a New Modernity*. SAGE. 53

Latour, B. 1996. On actor-network theory. A few clarifications plus more than a few complications. *Soziale Welt*, 47. 369-381. DOI: 10.22394/0869-5377-2017-1-173-197. 90, 104

Law, E. L-C. 2006. Evaluating the downstream utility of user tests and examining the developer effect: A case study. *International Journal of Human-Computer Interaction*, 21(2), 147–172. DOI: 10.1207/s15327590ijhc2102_3. 46, 75

Lawson, B. 1980. *How Designers Think*. Architectural Press. (2nd ed. 1990; 3rd 1998; 4th 2006). xvii, 13, 60, 69, 118

Löwgren, J. 1995. Applying design methodology to software development. *Proceedings Designing Interactive Systems (DIS '95)*, eds. Olson, G. M. and Schuon, S., ACM, 87–95. DOI: 10.1145/225434.225444. 24, 25, 26, 69, 70

Löwgren, J. 2013. Annotated portfolios and other forms of intermediate-level knowledge. *Interactions* 20(1), 30–34. DOI: 10.1145/2405716.2405725. 12, 28, 59, 62

Löwgren, J. and Stolterman, E. 2004. *Thoughtful Interaction Design: A Design Perspective on Information Technology*. MIT Press. 67

Maxcy, S. J. 2002. *Ethical School Leadership*. Rowman & Littlefield. 32

McDonald, S., Monahan, K., and Cockton, G. 2006. Using contextual design as a field evaluation method. In *Proceedings NordiCHI 2006*, eds. Mørch, A.I., Morgan, K., Bratteteig, T., Ghosh, G., and Svanæs, D., 437–440. DOI: 10.1145/1182475.1182531. xvi

McNeill, T., Gero, J. S., and Warren, J. 1998. Understanding conceptual electronic design using protocol analysis. *Research in Engineering Design*, 10(3),129–140. DOI: 10.1007/BF01607155. 14

McNeill, W. 1999. *The Glance of the Eye: Heidegger, Aristotle, and the Ends of Theory*. SUNY Press. 110

Mintzberg, H. 1994. *The Rise and Fall of Strategic Planning: Reconceiving Roles for Planning, Plans, Planners*. Free Press. 41, 42, 50

Mitchell, C. T. 1992. Preface to second edition, *Design Methods*, by Jones, J. C., Van Nostrand. ix–xi. 8

Mok, C. 1996. *Designing Business*. Hayden Books. 21

Moore, H. 1934. Statement for unit one. In *Unit One: The Modern Movement in English Architecture*, ed. Read, H., Cassell, 29–30. 65

Nelson, J. G. and Stolterman, E. 2003. *The Design Way: Intentional Change in an. Unpredictable World* (1st ed.). Educational Technology Publications. 107

Nelson, J. G. and Stolterman, E. 2012. *The Design Way: Intentional Change in an. Unpredictable World* (2nd ed.). MIT Press. DOI: 10.7551/mitpress/9188.001.0001. 13, 14, 16, 21, 24, 25, 27

Osterwalder, A., Pigneur, Y., Bernarda, G., Smith, A., and Papadakos, T. 2014. *Value Proposition Design: How to Create Products and Services Customers Want.* Wiley. 49, 66

Otero, N. and José, R. 2009. Worth and human values at the centre of designing situated digital public displays. *International Journal of Advanced Pervasive and Ubiquitous Computing (IJAPUC)*, 1(4), 1–13. DOI: 10.4018/japuc.2009100101. 67

Parnas D. L. and Clements P. C. 1986. A rational design process: how and why to fake it. *IEEE Transactions on Software Engineering*, 12(2), 251–257. DOI: 10.1109/TSE.1986.6312940. 31, 54, 74, 89, 92, 103, 117

Peirce, C. S. 1878. How to make our ideas clear. *Popular Science Monthly*, 12, 286–302. 22

Petre, M. and van der Hoek, A. 2016. *Software Design Decoded - 66 Ways Experts Think.* MIT Press. DOI: 10.7551/mitpress/10612.001.0001. 9

Petroski, H. 1994. *Design Paradigms: Case Histories of Error and Judgement in Engineering.* Cambridge University Press. DOI: 10.1017/CBO9780511805073. 17, 52, 54, 70

Plonka, L., Sharp, H., Gregory, P., and Taylor, K. 2014. UX design in agile: a DSDM case study. *Agile Processes in Software Engineering and Extreme Programming: 15th Int. Conf (XP 2014)*, Lecture Notes in Business Information Processing, LNBIP, vol. 179, 1–15. Springer. DOI: 10.1007/978-3-319-06862-6_1. 48

Poggenpohl, S. H. 2017. *Afterword Design and the Creation of Value*, eds. Dilnot, C. and Boztepe, S., 181. Bloomsbury. DOI: 10.5040/9781474274289.0021. 80, 85

Polya, G. 1945. *How To Solve It.* Princeton University Press. DOI: 10.1515/9781400828678. 53, 83

Popper, K. 1959. *The Logic of Scientific Discovery.* (author's translation of *Logik der Forschung*, 1934). Hutchinson, London. 60

Potter, N. 1989. *What Is a Designer: Things, Places, Messages*, 3rd ed., Hyphen Press. 65

Pye, D. 1968. *The Nature and Art of Workmanship.* Barrie and Jenkins. DOI: 10.2307/3101490. 15

Pye, D. 1978. *The Nature and Aesthetics of Design.* Barrie and Jenkins. 25

Quine, W. V. O. 1951. Two dogmas of empiricism. *The Philosophical Review*, 60, 20–43. DOI: 10.2307/2181906. 45

Rawls, J. 1971. *A Theory of Justice.* Harvard. 32

Renn, O. 1992. The social arena concept of risk debates. *Social Theories of Risk*, ed. Krimsky, S. Praeger, 179–196. 61, 63, 67, 78, 79, 86, 90, 105

Renn, O. 2008. *Risk Governance: Coping with Uncertainty in a Complex World*. Earthscan. DOI: 10.1007/978-1-4020-6799-0. xx

Rittel, H. W. J. and Webber, M. M. 1973. Dilemmas in a general theory of planning. *Policy Sciences*, 4, 155–169. DOI: 10.1007/BF01405730. 9, 14, 18, 25, 41, 54, 61, 76

Rogers, Y., Bannon, L., and Button, G. 1993. Rethinking theoretical frameworks for HCI: report on an INTERCHI '93 workshop, Amsterdam, April 24–25, 1993. *SIGCHI Bulletin*, 26(1), ACM, 28-30. DOI: 10.1145/181526.181530. xxi, 76

Rook, P. 1986. Controlling software projects. *Software Engineering Journal*, 1(1), 7–16. DOI: 10.1049/sej.1986.0003. 99, 100

Rylander, A. 2012. *Pragmatism and Design research—An overview*. Designfakultetens kunskapssammanställningar, Stockholm: KTH. Available from http://www.designfakulteten.kth.se/sites/default/files/designfpragdesignrapport_18.4.pdf. 44

Sauro, J. 2013. *Rating the Severity of Usability Problems*. https://measuringu.com/rating-severity/. 99

Schön, D. A. 1983. *The Reflective Practitioner: How Professionals Think in Action*. Basic Books. 25, 77, 85, 104

Schön, D. A. 1992. Designing as reflective conversation with the materials of a design situation. *Research in Engineering Design*, 3(1) 131–147. DOI: 10.1007/BF01580516. 12, 16, 17, 29, 109

Science Buddies. No Date. Comparing the Engineering Design Process and the Scientific Method. www.sciencebuddies.org/engineering-design-process/engineering-design-compare-scientific-method.shtml. 72

Siegel, D. and Dray, S. 2005. Avoiding the next schism: ethnography and usability. *Interactions*, 12(2), 58–61. DOI: 10.1145/1052438.1052469. 76

Siegel, D. and Dray, S. 2019. The map is not the territory: empathy in design. *Interactions*, 26(2), 82–85. DOI: 10.1145/3308647. 49

Simon, H. A. 1969. *The Sciences of the Artificial*, 1st ed., MIT Press. (2nd ed. 1981, 3rd ed. 1997). 77, 85

Stansfield, F. M. 1976. Models. *Engineering Design Guides*, 16. Oxford University Press. 73

Stebbing, L. S. 1930. *A Modern Introduction to Logic*. Methuen. 108

Steen, M. 2008. *The Fragility of Human-Centred Design*. IOS Press. 50

Stevens, J. and Moultrie, J. 2011. Aligning strategy and design perspectives: A framework of design's strategic contributions. *The Design Journal*, 14(4), 475–500. DOI: 10.2752/175630611X13091688930525. 12, 13, 15, 41, 66, 71, 99

Stewart, J. 2017. *Alvar Aalto, Architect*. Merrell. 22

Stolterman, E. 1999. The design of information systems: Parti, formats and sketching. Information Systems Journal, 9, 3-20. 125

Swartout, W. and Balzer, R. 1982. On the inevitable intertwining of specification and implementation. *CACM* 25(7), 438–440. DOI: 10.1145/358557.358572. 43

Takeuchi, H. and Nonaka, I. 1986. The new new product development game. *Harvard Business Review*, 64(1), 137–146. 13, 16, 17, 31, 41, 42, 48, 95, 114, 118

Thomas, J. C. and Carroll, J. M. 1979. The psychological study of design, *Design Studies*, 1(1), 5–11. DOI: 10.1016/0142-694X(79)90020-6. 23

Turns, J., Cuddihy, E., and Guan. Z. 2010. I thought this was going to be a waste of time: Using portfolio construction to support reflection on project-based experiences. *Interdisciplinary Journal of Problem-based Learning*, 4(2): 63–93. DOI: 10.7771/1541-5015.1125. 14

Umemoto, K., Endo, A., and Machado, M. 2004, From sashimi to zen-in: the evolution of concurrent engineering at Fuji Xerox. *Journal of Knowledge Management*, 8(4), 89–99. DOI: 10.1108/13673270410548504. 42, 51, 95

Von Hippel, E. 1986. Lead users: A source of novel product concepts. *Management Science*, 32 (7). 791–806. DOI: 10.1287/mnsc.32.7.791. 79

Vu, P. 2013. A Worth-Centered Development Approach to Information Management System Design. Master's Thesis, Aalto University. Available at: www.soberit.hut.fi/T-121/shared/thesis/di-Phuong-Vu.pdf. 124

Waloszek, G. 2012. *Introduction to Design Thinking*. SAP. https://experience.sap.com/skillup/introduction-to-design-thinking/. 29

Warfield, J.N., with Geschka, H. and Hamilton, R. 1975. Methods of Idea Management. The Academy for Contemporary Problems. 49

Weber, C. 2017. A note on John Heskett's economics. *Design and the Creation of Value*, eds. Dilnot, C. and Boztepe, S., Bloomsbury, 21–29. 16, 53

Weick, K. E. 1995. *Sensemaking in Organizations*. Sage. DOI: 10.1016/S0956-5221(97)86666-3. 109

Wetlaufer, S. 1997. What's stifling the creativity at CoolBurst? *Harvard Business Review*, 75(5), 36–40. 29

Whiteside, J., Bennett, J., and Holtzblatt, K. 1988. Usability engineering: Our experience and evolution. *Handbook of HCI*, ed. Helander, M. , 1st ed., North Holland, 791–817. DOI: 10.1016/B978-0-444-70536-5.50041-5. 76

Wolf, T. V., Rode, J. A., Sussman, J., and Kellogg, W. A. 2006. Dispelling "design" as the black art of CHI. *Proceedings SIGCHI Conference on Human Factors in Computing Systems. (CHI '06)*, eds. Grinter, R., Rodden, T., Aoki, P., Cutrell, E., Jeffries, R., and Olson, G., ACM, 521–530. DOI: 10.1145/1124772.1124853. 26, 27, 67, 80, 107

Woodruff, A. 2019. 10 things you should know about algorithmic fairness. *Interactions*, 26(4), 47–51. DOI: 10.1145/3328489. 17

Woolrych, A. Hornbæk, K. Frøkjær, E., and Cockton, G. 2011. Ingredients and meals rather than recipes: A proposal for research that does not treat usability evaluation methods as indivisible wholes. *International Journal of HCI*, 27(10), 940–970. DOI: 10.1080/10447318.2011.555314. 65

# Author Biography

Gilbert Cockton is a part-time Professorial Research Fellow at the University of Sunderland. He retired as Professor of Design Theory at Northumbria University in 2019, remaining affiliated with NORTH Lab as an Emeritus Professor. His career has balanced teaching, research, and working for and within businesses, government, and the third sector. He has worked in academic computing and design departments since 1984. From 2004, his research has focused on bringing critical creative practice fully and appropriately into software design and evaluation, first through value and worth as centres for design practice, and then through a generous Wo-Fo, progressing design work through balance and integration, developing approaches and resources that support realistic design practice.

Gilbert has held leadership roles in HCI groups in the British Computer Society, IFIP, and ACM, as chair of the BCS HCI group, vice-chair of IFIP TC13, programme co-ordinator for INTERACT'90, and general chair for CHI 2003 and British HCI 2000. He chaired ten technical tracks between 1993 and 2012 for the INTERACT, British HCI, CHI, and DIS conferences. He was co-editor in chief of ACM *Interactions* magazine from 2016–2019. He was awarded a SIGCHI Lifetime Service Award in 2020.

Printed in the United States
by Baker & Taylor Publisher Services